7 BASICS
strong roots for every christian

bethjones

Published By
Jeff and Beth Jones Ministries
www.jeffandbethjones.com

7 BASICS: Strong Roots for Every Christian
ISBN: 978-0-9851556-0-5

Copyright 2012 Beth Ann Jones
Published by Jeff and Beth Jones Ministries
P.O. Box 745, Portage, MI 49081
www.jeffandbethjones.com

Printed in the United States of America.

BOOKS BY BETH JONES

FAITH BASICS

The Spirit Empowered Life

SUCCESS BASICS

Wealth and Generosity

CLASSIC BASICS

7 Basics

Getting a Grip on the Basics

Getting a Grip on the Basics for Kids

Getting a Grip on the Basics for Teens

Getting a Grip on the Basics of Serving God

Getting a Grip on the Basics of Health and Healing

Getting a Grip on the Basics of Prosperous Living

Get a Grip on Your Lip

LIFE BASICS BIBLE STUDIES

BALANCE: Today's Christian Women Defined and Realigned

APPROVED: Getting a New View of You

ENERGY: Finding New Grace for the Pace

CLICK: Enjoyng Friendship for New Reasons and Seasons

BRAVE: Living a Fearless Life

UP: Writing a New Chapter of Joy and Laughter

BASIC QUESTIONS

Jesus: Is He Really the Only Way?

Hell: How Could a Loving God Send Anyone There?

CONTENTS

FIRST THINGS FIRST
JUST IN CASE YOU DON'T KNOW FOR SURE

Have faith in God; God has faith in you.
Edwin Louis Cole

Just in case you accidently found this book in your friend's apartment, under a bridge, in a trash can, on a park bench, in a taxi, in a palace, underneath your tip, in jail, at the doctor's office or in some other random place—and you aren't 100% sure you're a Christian or even what being a Christian or being "saved" means, let's take a moment to review the gospel to give you an opportunity to become a Christian!

GOD HAS A GREAT PLAN FOR YOUR LIFE

First, it starts with God's love for you! He has always had a great plan iin mind for you and your life. He's a good God and He loves you. All along it's been God's plan to bless you and give you a joyful, peace-filled, satisfying, fulfilling and abundant life. Jesus said, *"I have come that they may have life, and that they may have it more abundantly,"* *John 10:10, NKJV.*

Unfortunately, many people are not living in God's highest and best. They are not enjoying God's great plans and they are not experiencing the abundant life. There is a really good reason for that. Sin.

THE S WORD

We have a big problem! Sin. We've all blown it. Our sin has separated us from the God who loves us. It all started in the Garden of Eden when Adam and Eve ate that piece of fruit. You probably know the story.

7

After Creation, God made man and formed woman and then He gave them instructions on enjoying and guarding the Garden of Eden. Adam and Eve were filled with life, freedom, joy and abundance! There was only one restriction; they were not allowed to eat from the tree of the knowledge of good and evil. If they did so, God said they would die.

Meanwhile, before the Creation of man, one of God's heavenly angels had gone rogue and was cast out of heaven to earth. This fallen angel known as: the devil, Satan, Lucifer and the adversary came along in the form of a serpent to tempt Adam and Eve and turn their loyalties from God to his own voice. The devil wanted to be the boss. He wanted the allegiance of God's creation. So, he lied. He duped Adam and Eve with temptation and a lust for worldly, fleshly things and the promise of pride and glory. Sadly, they followed his direction and rebelled against God's words. They sinned by eating the fruit God had strictly forbidden.

THE FALL OF MAN WAS THE BIGGEST KIDNAPPING EVENT IN HISTORY. Little did they know the price their sin would require; that act of betrayal and rebellion towards God resulted in death—just like the Lord had said. They died spiritually that day and were separated from God—their physical death manifested some 900 years later. When Adam and Eve sinned, death entered earth and all of humanity. It was the most tragic day. Spiritual death and an eternal separation from God came upon the human race—mankind died. That's what the Bible is talking about when it says, *"The wages of sin is death,"* Romans 3:23, NKJV. Where life resounded, now death reigned. Mankind was lost. Cursed.

The fall of man was the biggest kidnapping event in history. Humanity was duped, hijacked, kidnapped and trafficked by following the deceiver's lies. Satan's goal has always been to steal, kill and destroy the very ones God had created. Through sin and the fall of man in the Garden, the enemy was successful in keeping mankind—including you and I— trapped in a life of perpetual sin and death that resulted in darkness, destruction, defeat and an eternal separation from God.

For thousands of years, humanity was lost and without hope in this world. There was a giant God-shaped hole within all of us. A great gulf separated us from the very One who created us. For thousands of years man tried to resolve this void and earn right standing with God through doing good deeds, establishing religious traditions or embracing philosophical theories. But at the end of the day, our best human efforts could not bridge the great eternal divide. We could not pay the ransom price to cover our sin and death. We could not earn God's forgiveness or favor. We could not fill the gap. We could not rescue ourselves. We were truly dead in our trespasses and sins and eternally separated from God.

JESUS TO THE RESCUE

God didn't leave us in that fallen condition. He wanted a relationship with us. When sin separated us from God and the enemy locked us up in his prison of death and darkness, the Lord did something to fix the problem—He sent Jesus to the rescue! The Bible spells it out, *"For God loved the world so much that he gave his one and only Son, so that everyone who believes in him will not perish but have eternal life,"* *John 3:16, NLT.*

Maybe you don't know much about Jesus—who He is and why He came. Perhaps, you've never known why you could or should believe in Him. Let me take a moment to introduce you to Jesus Christ.

JESUS IS THE GREATEST PERSON WHO HAS EVER LIVED.

Jesus is the greatest Person who has ever lived in all of Creation and in all of eternity. For those who look at historical evidence and the testimonies of eyewitnesses, the verdict is obvious. Jesus was and is God. He is the beginning and the end, the first and last, the Alpha and Omega, and the Author and Finisher of everything! Jesus is the eternal God and yet, He humbled Himself by stepping out of heaven to become a man and live on earth for thirty-three years. God put on human flesh and came to the planet He created.

While on earth, Jesus was the visible image of the invisible God. He loved people. He preached the truth. He went all over teaching, preaching and healing, to show people what God was like. He said that when people saw Him, they had seen the Father. He showed compassion. He did miracles. He raised the dead. He loved sinners. He healed the sick. He blessed children. He cared for the poor. He taught the Scriptures. He preached salvation. He cared about honesty, integrity and justice. He didn't like religious phonies. He called out hypocrites. He revealed the true nature of God. He went about doing good things and teaching people about the Father God.

Jesus was a good man and a great Teacher, but the primary reason Jesus came to earth *wasn't* to add His name to the list of well-known, religious leaders. The main reason Jesus came to earth was to rescue mankind and restore us back to God. He literally came to be our Savior—our Redeemer. He came to perform the most important and far-reaching search and rescue operation known to man.

Jesus was—and is—the only one qualified to fulfill such a mission. He is God—and man. As God, He humbled Himself and became a man. He was born as a baby in the manger, so He could die as our redeemer on the cross. He exchanged His sinless life for our sin-stained lives when He paid the ransom sin demanded with His spotless blood. He shed His blood for the forgiveness of our sin. *"For without the shedding of blood, there is no forgiveness," Hebrews 9:22, NLT.*

Jesus died on the cross for our sins. He paid the wage our sins demanded, but He didn't stay dead. Three days after His death on the cross, God raised Him from the dead. He is alive and seated in heaven. Jesus is not a dead religious leader; He is the living Savior of the world! It's no wonder Jesus said, *"I am the way, the truth, and the life. No one comes to the Father except through Me," John 14:6, NKJV.*

MAKE IT PERSONAL

HE WANTS TO HAVE A PERSONAL RELATIONSHIP WITH YOU.

Are you beginning to get a glimpse of how great God is? Can you see how much He loves you? Jesus is God's answer to the sin problem that plagued mankind. He is God's only provision for our sin. Jesus came to seek and save the lost. He came to forgive all our sins. He came to set us free. Jesus came so we could pass from death to life. He came to give us life more abundantly.

That's all great, right? Here's where it gets personal. God doesn't want Jesus to be an interesting biographical study, the subject of a lofty theological debate or an historical figure in a heady thesis on western civilization. God went to these great lengths because He wants to have a personal relationship with you.

10

This requires a decision on your part. It's not enough to know about Jesus, the gospel or Bible stories; you must make a personal decision to receive Jesus. God will never force Himself into your life; He gives you the choice to accept or reject His Son. He gives you the choice to turn from trusting in yourself—your own good works, religion and self-righteous acts—to trusting in Jesus.

Trusting Jesus and becoming a Christ-follower—a Christian—is not difficult. You simply put all of your trust in Jesus by believing, receiving, and invit-

DECLARE
JESUS AS THE
LORD OF YOUR LIFE.

ing Him into your heart. Declare Jesus as the Lord of your life. The result of trusting, believing, receiving and declaring Jesus as your Lord, is that you become a true-blue Christian!

If you have never invited Jesus to be the Lord of your life—please, take time to do so right now. Let's pray:

"Dear God, I want to become a Christian. I do believe and trust in Jesus. I believe He came to this earth to live a sinless life and to shed His blood on the cross for the forgiveness of my sin. I believe You raised Jesus from the dead and He is alive today. Jesus, I receive You into my life. Thank You for forgiving me of all of my sins. Today, I declare that Jesus Christ is the Lord of my life. I am saved. I am born again. I am a Christian! Amen."

DID I MENTION THE BIG JUDGMENT?

If you prayed this prayer, congratulations! It's a good thing, because I forgot to tell you about the judgment to come. While God is loving and full of mercy, He is also a God of justice and judgment and one day every person will stand before Him to give an account of their lives and choices.

The Apostle Paul said this, *"On that day when, as my Gospel proclaims, God by Jesus Christ will judge men in regard to the things which they conceal (their hidden thoughts),"* Romans 2:16, AMP. At the judgment, those who have rejected Jesus will find that their biggest sin and most notable deed is their choice to *not* trust, believe, receive or declare Jesus as Lord. Unfortunately, this choice will have grave eternal consequences.

11

The book of Revelation makes it clear, *"And I saw a great white throne and the one sitting on it. The earth and sky fled from his presence, but they found no place to hide. I saw the dead, both great and small, standing before God's throne. And the books were opened, including the Book of Life. And the dead were judged according to what they had done, as recorded in the books. The sea gave up its dead, and death and the grave gave up their dead. And all were judged according to their deeds. Then death and the grave were thrown into the lake of fire. This lake of fire is the second death. And anyone whose name was not found recorded in the Book of Life was thrown into the lake of fire,"* Revelation 20:11-15, NLT.

Thankfully, because of your decision to welcome Jesus into your life, when you stand before the Lord, you don't have to be afraid. With Jesus as your Lord, the Father will see you *in Him* and all of your sins washed in His blood. When you arrive at the Pearly Gates, there is just one *password*: *Jesus!*

THE PASSWORD:
JESUS

Your entrance into heaven might sound something like this: *"Thank You Heavenly Father for allowing me to enter Your eternal kingdom. I am so glad my name was written in Your Book of Life. I know that in and of myself, I have nothing to boast about. I don't deserve to be here, but Jesus is the Lord of my life. My trust is in Him and not in myself. On the cross Jesus took all my sins and He gave me His righteousness. He rose from the dead and is my Lord and Savior."* At about that time, God will smile at you and nod to a nearby angel who will take you to see your loved ones and give you a grand tour of heaven. Something like that.

If you have a Bible, I encourage you to look up these Scriptures.

SCRIPTURES TO READ

___ John 10:10
___ Romans 3:23, 6:23
___ Ephesians 2:1-4
___ John 14:6
___ Romans 10:9-10
___ 2 Corinthians 5:17-21
___ Revelation 20

INTRODUCTION

Faith is taking the first step
even when you don't see the whole staircase.
Martin Luther King, Jr.

Congratulations!

You get it! You are reading this book because somewhere along the way you welcomed Jesus into your life. You heard about Him and something clicked. You understood the gospel and you responded to God's invitation.

You may have invited Jesus into your heart moments ago, last week, two years or thirteen years ago. You may have surrendered to Jesus at church, after hearing a sermon or through an altar call. Maybe you prayed the salvation prayer or confessed Jesus as your Lord on your own, in a quiet way or in a moment of desperation. Everyone has a unique story. You may have turned to the Lord while reading the Bible or a Christian book. Perhaps, a family member, friend or coworker led you to the Lord. Maybe you heard the gospel at a concert, in the hospital or while in jail. You may have prayed to receive Jesus into your life after hearing the gospel online, on TV, through an audio message, a video clip or a download of some sort. Regardless of the path that led you to the Lord, surrendering to God and confessing Jesus, as the Lord of your life is the most important, life-transforming, eternal decision you will ever make.

It's my hope that through reading this book, God connects-the-dots for you on what it means to be a Christian. I pray your Christian life gets started (or restarted) on the right foot and you develop strong spiritual roots. As you read the *7 Basics*, may you gain a better understanding of God, Jesus, the Holy Spirit, God's love, the Bible, walking with the Lord, church, heaven, hell and all kinds of eternal things. May you truly get a grip on these basics and develop a passion to help others *get it*.

PARTY TIME

Before we get into the *7 Basics*, let's celebrate!

In case you didn't know, heaven is quite happy with your decision to believe in and receive Jesus. So thrilled, the angels threw a big party when you turned to the Lord. Listen to what Jesus said, *"Or imagine a woman who has ten coins and loses one. Won't she light a lamp and scour the house, looking in every nook and cranny until she finds it? And when she finds it you can be sure she'll call her friends and neighbors: 'Celebrate with me! I found my lost coin!' Count on it—that's the kind of party God's angels throw every time one lost soul turns to God,"* Luke 15:8-10, MSG.

GOD'S ANGELS
THROW A PARTY!

If you haven't yet taken time to celebrate and document when you came to know Jesus, do it now. Write down the details of the day you confessed Jesus as Lord.

Your Name:_____

Day/Date/Time:_____

Where:_____

Witnesses:_____

YOU GOT A DO-OVER

Now that Jesus is the Lord of your life, everything has changed! Your life was reset. More than that, your life was reinvented—literally recreated! Jesus gave you a second chance—a complete do-over! A real miracle occurred in your life when Jesus moved into you heart. You may not know the magnitude of this do-over yet, but in time, you'll see it clearly.

If you think about it, yesterday, you may have been a low-down, rotten, no-good sinner; you may have been agnostic, atheist, anti-Christ or apathetic towards God. You may have been the biggest partier on campus, the most promiscuous girl in your workplace or the bad-to-the-bone guy in your circle of friends. Maybe your sins were a mile high and you thought you were unworthy of God's love—but now you know, you weren't too far away to receive Jesus and His mercy.

At the other extreme, you may have been the nicest person in your world and the most pure-as-the-driven-snow, goody-two-shoes ever known. You may have given money to charity, housed the homeless and marched for every cause you believed in. You might have been a religious, churchgoer that didn't miss a single Sunday service. Maybe your good deeds and religious pedigree were a thousand acres deep and you figured you were doing a pretty good job trusting in your own good efforts—but now you know, you weren't good enough to live without Jesus and His mercy.

The truth be told; we all need Jesus. WE ALL NEED JESUS! He came from heaven to earth, to die on a cross to give us a complete do-over—the worst among us and the best among us.

THE BIGGEST PIVOT POINT

When you turned from your own ways to the Lord, He came running with His love and mercy. This was the biggest pivot point of your life. When you believed in Jesus and received Him into your life by faith, He pardoned and removed all of your sins, exchanged your attempts to be self-righteous with His perfect righteousness and welcomed you into His family as His very own child.

Listen to this, *"He has removed our sins as far from us as the east is from the west,"* Psalm 103:12, NLT. He said He would not remember them any longer. He didn't just forgive and remove your sins. He actually changed your status. God has acquitted you of every sin, pronounced you *not guilty* and made you *righteous* in His eyes. *"This righteousness is given through faith in Jesus Christ to all who believe,"* Romans 3:22, NIV. Your sins are gone. You've been made righteous. What a gift! In God's eyes, because of Jesus and His work on the cross, you have been reconciled to God. You can stand before God just as if you have never sinned.

What does this mean? According to God's view, it means: you're a true Christian. You're a believer. You've been born again. You're saved. You've been redeemed. You're a follower of Jesus. You're a friend of God. What do all of these things *really* mean? They mean you have become a new person and your eternal destination has been rerouted. Before you accepted or confessed Jesus as your Lord, you were separated from God because of your sin. You were lost and taking a one-way trip to an eternal separation from God in a terrible place called hell.

HE SAVED YOU AND RESET YOUR ETERNAL DESTINATION.

Because of God's love and mercy—when you received Jesus, He saved you and reset your eternal destination to heaven! God wrote your name in the Book of Life—His reservation book in Heaven.

Does this sound familiar? *"It wasn't so long ago that you were mired in that old stagnant life of sin. You let the world, which doesn't know the first thing about living, tell you how to live. You filled your lungs with polluted unbelief, and then exhaled disobedience. We all did it, all of us doing what we felt like doing, when we felt like doing it, all of us in the same boat. It's a wonder God didn't lose his temper and do away with the whole lot of us. Instead, immense in mercy and with an incredible love, he embraced us. He took our sin-dead lives and made us alive in Christ. He did all this on his own, with no help from us! Then he picked us up and set us down in highest heaven in company with Jesus, our Messiah," Ephesians 2:1-6, MSG.*

Not only is your eternal destination secure, the rest of your life on earth has the potential to be very different because of Jesus and His gift of salvation. You are in for an exciting adventure as you get to know the Lord and walk with Him. So, what now?

THE LEARNING CURVE

Whenever you start anything new, there is a learning curve. Whether you're an athlete or a new employee, there is a learning curve to master. If you're visiting a foreign country, trying to understand a new computer program or figuring out how to use an app on your phone, there's going to be a time period of learning. There are new words to memorize; new people to meet; new things to discover and new processes and systems to understand.

The same thing is true in your new relationship with the Lord. From the time you are born again until you become a fully functional mature believer, there is a learning curve. Getting to know God is just like getting to know a new Person! This takes time. There's a whole new glossary of Bible words to learn. There are many new spiritual things to discover. Fortunately, you have the best teacher in all of Creation—God Himself, Who will take you by the hand and help you to learn.

PUT DOWN ROOTS

Think about this spiritual learning curve like you would think about caring for a very precious plant. You are that plant! Through being attentive, patient and focused on the right things you can grow a healthy, fruitful plant with deep roots. In the same way, as you give your attention to the *7 Basics*, focusing on the content and Scriptures in each chapter, you will grow into a very beautiful, healthy, fruitful Christian with strong roots firmly planted in God.

Remember, getting rooted in the Lord takes time. You will have questions about God and you may feel like you should know more than you do; be patient. You won't have all the answers overnight. It will take time for you to grow in your knowledge of God, but as you get started, you will sense your spiritual roots growing and getting stronger in the Lord.

Always keep this in mind; if you want a big life with God, you will need deep roots! It takes a lot of time—up to several decades—to grow a large, stately oak tree with a strong root system as its

IF YOU WANT A BIG LIFE WITH GOD YOU WILL NEED DEEP ROOTS!

foundation. It takes less than a month to grow a full-sized mushroom; however, a mushroom's root system is very shallow. In order to have a root system like a majestic oak tree, rather than the shallow roots of a mushroom fungus, you will need to carve out time to get to know the Lord.

A friend of mine, and her husband, own a large greenhouse operation and she told me some very interesting things about the art of growing plants. She said that they can "force grow" a plant by using certain techniques, but they have to be very careful otherwise the plant will grow too quickly and have a few fatal flaws.

First, if the growth is forced too quickly, the plant will never produce fruit. Isn't that sad, a plant that is supposed to produce fruit will never develop any! Second, if they accelerate the growth too much, the root system will not have a chance to develop properly. If this plant were to be transplanted to a natural outdoor environment, it would likely not survive because it did not have time to develop hearty roots that could withstand winds, storms and a harsh environment.

What a great analogy for the growth and development of your life as a Christian. God won't "force grow" your life. He wants you to produce fruit and He wants you to have hearty roots so that you can survive and thrive in the harsh elements of this world. Give yourself an advantage and take time to allow for healthy, balanced spiritual growth.

Psalm 1 is a great description of what God has in store for you as you get rooted in the basics. *"Oh, the joys of those who do not follow the advice of the wicked, or stand around with sinners, or join in with mockers. But they delight in the law of the LORD, meditating on it day and night. They are like trees planted along the riverbank, bearing fruit each season. Their leaves never wither, and they prosper in all they do,"* Psalm 1:1-3, NLT.

GET STARTED

To get started, I encourage you to do these things: Pray. Invest. Do.

PRAY.
INVEST.
DO.

Pray and Ask God For Help: As a new or young believer, you are not expected to know everything about God and you are not expected to do the Christian life perfectly in the first ten minutes. Ask the Lord to help you and He will!

Invest 15 Minutes a Day: As you begin your life with Jesus, invest 15 minutes into your relationship with the Lord. Here's an easy way to get started doing this: Each day, read a portion of this *7 Basics* book and then look up every verse in the **Scriptures to Read** section mentioned at the end of each chapter. (We'll talk about what versions of the Bible you should have when we get to Basic #2—so for now, use whatever Bible you have.) If you will invest fifteen minutes daily, I believe you will sense the Lord speaking to you and your relationship with Him will become very real to you. Don't be in a hurry. Take your time as you read, reflect, ponder and meditate on the things God is speaking to your heart.

Do What You Learn: Most people learn best by doing. The Bible tells us it's the doers of the Word who are blessed, not just the hearers. So, as you get into God's Word, ask the Lord to show you how to put the things you are learning into practice. Then do it!

THE 7 BASICS

Are you ready to go? You've probably heard of the Seven Wonders of the World, a seven-layer salad and the top seven drinks at Starbucks, but now it's time to get acquainted with the *7 Basics!* Turn up your expectation and prepare to be enlightened, encouraged, challenged, inspired and stretched as you get into these seven very important basics:

TURN UP YOUR EXPECTATION!

BASIC #1: Get To Know God
BASIC #2: Get Into The Bible
BASIC #3: Get Real In Prayer
BASIC #4: Get Into A Good Church
BASIC #5: Get Excited And Tell Somebody
BASIC #6: Get Your Head On Straight
BASIC #7: Get Ready For The Adventure

This is my prayer for you as you get started in the *7 Basics; "I pray that from His glorious, unlimited resources He will empower you with inner strength through his Spirit. Then Christ will make His home in your hearts as you trust in Him. Your roots will grow down into God's love and keep you strong. And may you have the power to understand, as all God's people should, how wide, how long, how high, and how deep His love is. May you experience the love of Christ, though it is too great to understand fully. Then you will be made complete with all the fullness of life and power that comes from God. Now all glory to God, who is able, through his mighty power at work within us, to accomplish infinitely more than we might ask or think," Ephesians 3:16-20, NLT.*

SCRIPTURES TO READ

___ Psalm 1
___ John 3:1-17
___ Luke 15:8-10

BASIC #1
GET TO KNOW GOD

What were we made for? To know God.
What aim should we have in life? To know God.
What is the eternal life that Jesus gives? To know God.
What is the best thing in life? To know God.
J. I. Packer

When a couple pledges their wedding vows and says, "I do"—those words aren't the end of the relationship, they're just the beginning. That young bride or groom doesn't say, *"Well, I did it. I said 'I do'—now I'll just go back to living the way I used to live as a single person."* No! That commitment and those vows are the beginning of a new relationship. After the "I do's"—that married couple can really get to know one another intimately.

The same thing is true in your relationship with the Lord. When you welcomed Jesus to be the Lord of your life, it marked the beginning of your vow. Now that you've said, "I do," let's get this relationship started!

HE IS THAT INTO YOU

Some people may not be that into you, but God is very into you! He knit you together in your mother's womb. He wanted you. He knows the number of hairs on your head. He knows when you wake up and when you go to sleep. His eyes are always on you. He orders your steps. He knows your thoughts before you do.

He knows all about you; but He wants to be known—by you. He is knowable and He wants to have a close, personal, heart-felt relationship with you. What do you know about Him? He knows all about you, but how well do you know Him? What is He like? How does He think? What are His favorite things? If you don't instinctively see Him as a God of love, mercy, goodness, kindness, favor, faithfulness, generosity, truth or holiness—among many of His characteristics—you are in for a nice surprise.

People have all kinds of unbiblical ideas about God. Some think He's a far-off, uninterested, detached Being. Some people see Him as a mean Judge ready to slam them for their sins. Others see Him as a wimpy, spineless Being; a cotton candy God of love that just winks at everything. Some people see God as an uncaring, sovereign ruler who causes bad things to happen to good people; or as a ruthless, yet somehow *all-wise* God who punishes and abuses people to teach them lessons.

Don't let the opinion of others, or even your own ideas or experiences define God for you; let the Lord reveal Himself to you. The primary way God reveals the truth about Himself to us is through His Word. As you spend time with the Lord and reading the Bible, He will become more and more real to you.

Don't ever forget, being a Christian is not about being religious or following some letter-of-the-law set of rules—it's about having a personal relationship with Jesus—the real, loving, living God! It's about knowing the God of the Bible who put on flesh and dwelt among us. He is the Almighty, the Creator of the ends of the earth, the Most High God, and most notably, your Father, your Friend and your Helper. Getting to know the Lord is all about learning, walking, talking, listening, sharing, following, asking and doing life with the One who loves you deeply.

SPEND TIME WITH THE LORD.

Knowing God the Father and Jesus Christ through the help of the Holy Spirit is what it is all about. Jesus made it crystal clear, *"And this is eternal life, that they may know You, the only true God, and Jesus Christ whom You have sent," John 17:3, NKJV.*

How do you get to know the Lord? Like any relationship, it starts by spending time together. One of the best ways to get started is by setting aside a daily quiet time to spend alone with the Lord. Jesus made a practice of this, often getting up in the early morning, to spend time with the Father. During your quiet time, you can read the Bible and allow God to talk to you, then pray and talk to the Lord about all kinds of things. You will always leave your quiet time with the Lord at peace and refreshed, comforted, enlightened, challenged, corrected, encouraged and strengthened for the day.

YOU'VE BEEN ADOPTED

When Jesus became the Lord of your life, several supernatural things happened. One big event that transpired was your official adoption into God's family. *"God decided in advance to adopt us into his own family by bringing us to himself through Jesus Christ. This is what he wanted to do, and it gave him great pleasure," Ephesians 1:5, NLT.*

It gave Him pleasure to adopt you. He picked you. Ponder that for a while! Not only that, you began an eternal, faith-filled adventure with the Lord. He has a great plan for your life, a divine purpose for your future. He wants to give you His wisdom and guidance. God wants your life to be   HE PICKED YOU! satisfying, significant, influential and fa- vored. He wants to bless you and make you a blessing. He wants to do things in you and through you. You may not know it yet, but you've been adopted into a very loving, generous and influential family—the family of God. As you walk closely with the Lord, you will experience the blessings that come with being in His family. Not only that, He will work through you to bless those around you, to impact generations to come and to put a big dent in eternity.

Let's explore what it means to get to know God—the Father, Son and Holy Spirit.

THREE IN ONE?

Have you ever been confused by the various words we use for God? We call Him: God, Father, Jesus, Lord, Holy Spirit—but what do all of these words mean? When we use the word "God"—Who are we talking about?

In the Bible, God has literally revealed Himself as the Godhead (or what some people refer to as the Trinity). The Godhead, or Trinity, is simply God revealing Himself in three persons: God the Father, God the Son and God the Holy Spirit.

The Lord our God is one God, revealed in three Persons. The Godhead

23

is not three Gods, revealed in one Person. The Godhead is One God, revealed in three Persons. Let's look at a few Scriptures to better understand this reality.

"Hear, O Israel: The LORD our God, the LORD is one! You shall love the LORD your God with all your heart, with all your soul, and with all your strength," Deuteronomy 6:4-5, NKJV. Our one God is revealed in three Persons, *"For there are three that bear witness in heaven: the Father, the Word, and the Holy Spirit; and these three are one,"* 1 John 5:7, NKJV.

One God, three Persons. What does that mean to you and me? It means that we get to know the multi-faceted, rich dimensions of our one God (the Godhead) by getting to know the Person of God the Father, the Person of Jesus our Lord and the Person of the Holy Spirit. All the fullness of the Godhead dwells in Jesus—so as we especially focus walking with Jesus, we will truly get to know God.

"As you therefore have received Christ Jesus the Lord, so walk in Him, rooted and built up in Him and established in the faith, as you have been taught, abounding in it with thanksgiving. Beware lest anyone cheat you through philosophy and empty deceit, according to the tradition of men, according to the basic principles of the world, and not according to Christ. For in Him dwells all the fullness of the Godhead bodily," Colossians 2:6-9, NKJV.

IT WILL TAKE ALL OF ETERNITY TO GET TO KNOW GOD.

7 BASICS ABOUT GOD

It will take all of eternity to get to know God. To give you a snapshot of your great God, let's look at these seven truths and then we will spend some time getting to know the Father, Jesus and the Holy Spirit personally and individually.

God is love. 1 John 4:8
The Father is good all the time. Matthew 7:11
The Father is on your side. Romans 8:31
Jesus is Lord. Philippians 2:6-11
Jesus gives you His peace. John 16:33
The Holy Spirit helps you. John 14:16, 26, 16:13
The Holy Spirit gives you power. Acts 1:8

GET TO KNOW THE FATHER

God, the Father is the first Person of the Godhead. He is your true Father. Sure, He is all-powerful (omnipotent), all-knowing (omniscient) and present everywhere (omnipresent), but one of the most wonderful things Jesus showed us about God is that He is our Father. *"See how very much our Father loves us, for he calls us his children, and that is what we are!" 1 John 3:1, MSG.* When you stop and think about this, it is quite profound. He is truly the Father of you—the real you!

Can you think of any human fathers—including your own father—who you admire, respect and enjoy being around? God is a father like that—only a million times more so!

As your Father, He loves you and has always loved you. He wants you and has always wanted you. He accepts you and has always accepted you. He is interested in your life and has always been interested in you. He wants the best for you and has always wanted the best for you. He is a good Father and He is a giving Father. He is a caring Father and He corrects us for our good. Your Heavenly Father wants to spend time with you, to talk with you, to teach you and to guide you. He cares about you.

HE LOVES YOU AND HAS ALWAYS LOVED YOU.

In fact, God has such a Father's heart, Jesus told us that one of the very reasons He came to earth was to reconcile us back to the Father. *Jesus said, "...No one comes to the Father except through Me," John 14:6, NKJV.* Jesus came so we could have access to the Father.

Sometimes, it's hard for people to grasp what it means to have a loving Heavenly Father. There are several reasons for our misconstrued ideas. Let's look at a few:

Do you see God as a mean Judge? You may have heard, been taught or received ideas about God that were not true or biblical. Some people have been taught that God is a mean judge who sits up in heaven ready to pour out His wrath on us for the slightest thing. The opposite is true! He is rich in mercy and He loved us when we were far from Him. In His loving-kindness, He patiently drew us to Jesus so that through Him, we could experience forgiveness, grace and the fullness of our Father's goodness.

Do you have a complex relationship with your human father? You may have had a difficult, complicated or painful relationship with your earthly father—and you may have felt *fatherless* during your life. The role of our earthly father is very significant and if you did not have a good experience with your dad, you can unknowingly picture your Heavenly Father to be similar to your earthly father.

If you have a difficult time embracing the idea of a loving Heavenly Father, or if you've felt rejected, abandoned, disapproved, unloved, unwanted and even abused by your earthly father, your Heavenly Father wants to reverse those things. He wants to reveal Himself to you in a way that is completely opposite of the ungodly things you have experienced.

The Father doesn't just love you in a theoretical way. He loves you so much He demonstrated it by sending Jesus. *"But God demonstrates His own love toward us, in that while we were still sinners, Christ died for us," Romans 5:8, NKJV.* When He sent Jesus to earth to save you—it was because He loves you!

There are so many facets to knowing God as your Father; experiencing His love and drawing close to Him will take all of eternity! Your journey in getting to know your Heavenly Father will be one of the most exciting parts of your Christian life.

GET TO KNOW JESUS

Jesus is the second Person of the Godhead. The most important thing to know about Jesus is simply this: He loves you! Are you seeing a theme? God is love. He loved you when you were far from Him and He loves you now. Everything about Jesus and why He came to earth has to do with His love for you. He is motivated towards you by love. He responds to you in love. He is love. Don't ever forget that simple fact.

HE IS LOVE.

However, just because He is love doesn't mean He is spineless mush, quite the opposite in fact. Because He loves you perfectly, He speaks the truth to you. He corrects you when needed. He won't let you live in peace when you are heading in the wrong direction. He doesn't let you have your way, when your desires are not aligned with His purposes for you. His love is pure, completely unselfish and He always desires what is best for you.

During Jesus' earthly ministry, compassion moved Him to go throughout cities, towns and villages teaching the truth, preaching the good news, healing sick people, performing miracles, walking on water, multiplying food, rebuking the devil, calling out religious hypocrites, blessing children, helping those in need and revealing the Father God to all who would listen and believe. Jesus was so wonderful multitudes walked miles upon miles to hear Him and to be near Him. This was before texting, Facebook and Twitter! In order for the multitudes to know where to gather and find Jesus, He must have had a compelling reputation for love, compassion and truth. Thankfully, He's still the same today, *"Jesus Christ is the same yesterday, today, and forever,"* Hebrews 13:8, NKJV.

JESUS IS STILL THE SAME.

Let's take a more in depth look at Jesus, so you can get to know Him in a very personal way. Jesus is God. He has always existed. Jesus was with the Father in the beginning and through Him the world was created. Jesus humbled Himself, put on the human body God has prepared for Him and came to earth. He was the Son of God and the Son of Man. He was born to a Virgin named Mary and He lived on earth for thirty-three years. The Bible tells us a little bit about those thirty-three years. He was raised in a Jewish home. He obeyed his parents. He loved His mother. He was the son of a carpenter. He had several brothers and sisters. He was a student of the Word. He studied the Old Testament, especially the Torah.

Jesus knew who He was and why He came. He didn't reveal Himself to the world until He was around thirty years old. After John the Baptist baptized Him in the Jordan River, Jesus began His ministry and disclosed Himself to those who would receive Him. He showed Himself to be the great *I am*. He told his followers that He was the visible image of the invisible God. He was Immanuel—God with us. Jesus was and is the Messiah—the anointed One!

At the right time, Jesus laid down His very life to give us the abundant life He promised. No one took His life; He laid it down freely because Jesus said, *"The Son of Man must be delivered into the hands of sinful men, and be crucified, and the third day rise again,"* Luke 24:7, NKJV.

27

He knew that the biggest part of His mission on earth was to shed His blood for the forgiveness of our sins. Jesus carried the weight of our sins—the sins of the whole world—when He went to the cross. He shed His blood and paid the wage of death our sins demanded.

On the cross, Jesus identified with us in our sin, so that we could identify with Him and all that He is. This is sometimes called *the great exchange*. *"I have been crucified with Christ; it is no longer I who live, but Christ lives in me; and the life which I now live in the flesh I live by faith in the Son of God, who loved me and gave Himself for me,"* Galatians *2:20, NKJV.*

After Jesus died, He went to hell in our place. There, He defeated the devil and took the keys of death, hell and the grave; and then God raised Jesus from the dead! The resurrection of Jesus Christ was the most powerful event in human history. Hell shook as the power of His resurrection reversed the curse and opened the door of salvation and redemption for all mankind! Jesus rewound thousands of years of human history when He paid the wages of sin—past, present and future—with His own death. Through the cross and resurrection, Jesus opened the door for mankind to experience real life. Jesus made that clear when He said, *"I came that they may have and enjoy life, and have it in abundance (to the full, till it overflows),"* John 10:10, AMP.

Today, Jesus is alive! He is seated at the Father's right hand in heaven. He has been given all power and all authority. He has the Name above every name. He is the King of kings and the Lord of lords. He is our Lord and Savior. He is our Redeemer, Friend and Brother. He is the Light of the world. He is our Prince of Peace, our Good Shepherd, our Healer and so much more! Jesus is our Hero and He's coming again!

KNOWING ABOUT JESUS IS GREAT, BUT KNOWING JESUS IS BETTER.

Knowing *about* Jesus is great, but *knowing* Jesus is better. The minute Jesus became the Lord of your life, you became the *real time* recipient of a *great salvation* which includes: friendship with God, joy and peace, the riches of His mercy, great grace and favor, forgiveness and right standing with God. You became an heir of every blessing that originates in heaven. You received the power of attorney to use the Name of Jesus in prayer. You've been given the armor of God to overcome every fiery dart that comes against you and the Word of God to give you the victory in every battle—and so much more. Jesus meant it when He promised to give us an abundant life—to the full until it overflows! Can you see how thrilling it is to know Him personally?

GET TO KNOW THE HOLY SPIRIT

The Holy Spirit is the third Person of the Godhead. He is not a power, vapor or force, He is a Person. He is just as much God as the Father and Jesus.

Jesus told His disciples—and us—that after He died on the cross and rose from the dead, He would not leave us as orphans, but He would send One just like Him. He did, He sent the Holy Spirit.

One of the roles of the Holy Spirit is to draw us to Jesus. Do you remember His work in your own life? It was the Holy Spirit—the Helper—who was at work getting your attention, convincing your heart and revealing Jesus to you. Listen to what Jesus said, *"Nevertheless I tell you the truth. It is to your advantage that I go away; for if I do not go away, the Helper will not come to you; but if I depart, I will send Him to you. And when He has come, He will convict the world of sin, and of righteousness, and of judgment: of sin, because they do not believe in Me; of righteousness, because I go to My Father and you see Me no more; of judgment, because the ruler of this world is judged,"* John 16:7-11, NKJV.

GETTING TO KNOW THE HOLY SPIRIT IS A JOYOUS ADVENTURE.

When you welcomed Jesus to be your Lord and invited Him to *come into your heart*—He didn't physically shrink and move into your heart. However, He did come to live inside of you through the presence of the Holy Spirit.

Getting to know the Holy Spirit is a joyous adventure. His role in your life is multi-faceted. As you get to know Him, you will recognize His work. He is the one who continually reveals Jesus to you. He makes the Bible come alive. He leads and guides you with His still small voice. He teaches you what is true and He shows you things to come. In fact, in the same way that the disciples walked and talked with Jesus while wearing leather sandals and traveling on dusty trails; Jesus made it possible—through the help of the Holy Spirit—for you to walk and talk with Him while carrying coffee-filled cups and traveling the busy roads around you.

Jesus told us what we could expect. *"I still have many things to say to you, but you cannot bear them now. However, when He, the Spirit of truth, has come, He will guide you into all truth; for He will not speak on His own authority, but whatever He hears He will speak; and He will tell you things to come. He will glorify Me, for He will take of what is Mine and declare it to you. All things that the Father has are Mine. Therefore I said that He will take of Mine and declare it to you,"* John 16:7-15, NKJV.

THE HOLY SPIRIT IS YOUR HELPER.

The Spirit is truly your Helper, Guide, Comforter, Counselor, Strengthener, Defense Attorney and Prayer Partner. Jesus described Him this way, *"...I will ask the Father, and He will give you another Comforter (Counselor, Helper, Intercessor, Advocate, Strengthener, and Standby), that He may remain with you forever—The Spirit of Truth, Whom the world cannot receive (welcome, take to its heart), because it does not see Him or know and recognize Him. But you know and recognize Him, for He lives with you [constantly] and will be in you,"* John 14:16-17, AMP.

Not only does the Holy Spirit live within you, God wants you to be filled with the Spirit! Being filled with the Spirit will give you the power you need to live for Christ and He will produce good fruit in your life, *"But the Holy Spirit produces this kind of fruit in our lives: love, joy, peace, patience, kindness, goodness, faithfulness, gentleness, and self-control,"* Galatians 5:22-23, NLT.

You should know that because a believer can be *filled* with the Spirit; by default it is also possible to be *half-full* or *just above empty*. Jesus told us that every believer should be filled, baptized or immersed in the Holy Spirit. That means no part of the person is left untouched; they are entirely pervaded, thoroughly permeated and wholly enveloped by the Holy Spirit. Think about that. Open your heart up to God and seek, ask for and receive all that the Holy Spirit has for you. Jesus said it this way, *"And don't you think the Father who conceived you in love will give the Holy Spirit when you ask him?"* Luke, 11:13, MSG. Make this your daily expectation and heart pursuit. 30

KNOWING GOD

People who know God experience real life. Those who truly get to know God the Father, Jesus the Lord and the Holy Spirit have reported these kinds of things:

"Knowing God gave me peace—a wonderful, quiet, steady, deep peace."

"It was like being flooded with joy."

"I found my priorities in life were completely altered."

"His presence made me happy and free."

"I just had an insatiable desire to pray, worship and go to church."

"I passionately wanted to avoid anything that would offend Him."

"He made me feel like I was made brand new all over again."

"He makes me want to tell everyone about God."

I hope you are sensing the joy of what it means to get to know God—Father, Son and Holy Spirit. He has promised if we seek, crave and require Him with our whole hearts, we will find Him in very personal ways.

"Seek, inquire of and for the Lord, and crave Him and His strength (His might and inflexibility to temptation); seek and require His face and His presence [continually] evermore," Psalm 105:4, AMP.

SCRIPTURES TO READ

___ Psalm 25
___ Psalm 27
___ Psalm 105
___ Matthew 5-6
___ Philippians 3:10
___ Matthew 3:11-12
___ Acts 1:4-5
___ John 14-17

STUDY GUIDE

Please review the previous chapter and use this Study Guide to journal the things you are learning about God.

1. Based upon what you just read, if you had to describe God in ten words, what ten words would you use?

2. When you think of getting to know God as your Father, what things about Him do you most look forward to experiencing?

3. When you think about getting to know Jesus better, what things about Him stand out to you?

4. When you think about getting to know the Holy Spirit, what do you most look forward to?

5. Write a short note to the Lord and tell Him what He means to you.

BASIC #2
GET INTO THE BIBLE

A thorough knowledge of the Bible
is worth more than a college education.
Theodore Roosevelt

The God of the Universe wants to talk to you! That ought to get your attention. God has things to say. The Lord wants to load you up with His Word. A huge treasure of wisdom, knowledge, understanding, revelation and faith awaits you as you start reading the Bible!

A LOVE LETTER, A MAP AND AN OWNER'S MANUAL

Have you ever loved someone so much that you just had to tell them? Have you ever written or received a love letter? How did you feel when you read words that were written just to you—so you would know how much you are loved?

How about a map? Ever needed your GPS to map out the route for a big road trip? How about an owner's manual? Ever read an owner's manual so you could operate all the options on your new car or technological toy?

God's Word—the Bible—is His personal love letter to you! It's His map—His global positioning system—for living. It's the owner's manual for every option in life. The Bible is God's living Word. When you read the Bible, God talks to your heart!

Sometimes people hope God will talk to them through a booming voice from the sky, or by writing on a billboard that comes floating down from heaven. God wants to speak to you, but in most cases, He won't speak to you through booming voices or billboards from heaven.

The primary way God speaks today is through His Word—the Bible. Through spending time reading the Bible, you will get to know the Lord. You will hear Him speaking to your heart and you find out how much He loves you. You will find the route He wants your life to take. You will learn how to access all the options He's given you for driving through life. Let's take a look at the Bible.

THE BIBLE IS A SUPERNATURAL BOOK

The Bible is a supernatural book. It is unlike any other book on earth. It is alive! *"For the word of God is alive and powerful. It is sharper than the sharpest two-edged sword, cutting between soul and spirit, between joint and marrow. It exposes our innermost thoughts and desires,"* Hebrews 4:12, NLT.

There are two parts to the Bible: the Old Testament and the New Testament. The Old Testament describes God's laws, prophecies and dealings with the Jewish people before Jesus was born. The Old Testament points forward to the time when Messiah, would come to save God's people from their sin. The New Testament reveals Jesus as the Messiah and details His life, ministry, death on the cross, resurrection and His coming again. The New Testament documents the age of grace revealed through Jesus Christ as well as the birth of His Church and purposes until He comes again.

THE BIBLE IS UNLIKE ANY BOOK ON EARTH.

There are sixty-six books in the Bible. Forty different authors who had various occupations wrote the Bible. It was written during a period of 1500 years in three languages—Hebrew, Aramaic and Greek. The Bible has one consistent theme in both Old and New Testaments: Jesus Christ. The Bible is not a natural book. It is obvious to any reader that there is one Supreme Author of the Bible, the Holy Spirit of God. He inspired the prophets of old to convey His words: *"Above all, you must realize that no prophecy in Scripture ever came from the prophet's own understanding, or from human initiative. No, those prophets were moved by the Holy Spirit, and they spoke from God,"* 2 Peter 1:20-21, NLT.

It's true. The Bible is a God-inspired book. *"All Scripture is inspired by God and is useful to teach us what is true and to make us realize what is wrong in our lives. It corrects us when we are wrong and teaches us to do what is right,"* 2 Timothy 3:16, NLT.

When you read the Bible, the Holy Spirit makes it come alive in your heart. Through reading God's Word, the Lord will speak to you and give you wisdom, knowledge, understanding and insights. He will reveal things to you. He will tell you secrets. He will guide you. He will give you information you need to know.

FIRST STEP: GET A BIBLE

Everyone needs a Bible. The first and most important thing to do as you get to know the Lord personally is to get a Bible and begin reading it. You might wonder, what type of Bible should you get?

EVERYONE NEEDS A BIBLE.

There are several types of Bibles and it's helpful to understand the differences between them. One important thing to recognize is the difference between a *translation* of the Bible and a *paraphrase* of the Bible.

A translation of the Bible is more closely aligned with the original manuscripts as it has been translated from the original languages (Hebrew, Greek, Aramaic) into English. A Bible translation is a more accurate version of the Bible. You will definitely want to get a good Bible translation to read and study.

A paraphrase Bible is simply that—a paraphrase of the translation. The authors of the paraphrase Bibles did their best to paraphrase the meaning of the words to make the Bible more modern and readable. A paraphrased Bible is fun to read for a fresh perspective, but it is not the type of Bible you want to use for detailed study.

7 BIBLES TO CONSIDER

Here are seven versions of the Bible you may want to add to your personal library.

Widely Recognized Translations of the Bible

King James Version (KJV)
New King James Version (NKJV)
New International Version (NIV)
Amplified Bible Classic (AMPC)
New Living Translation (NLT)

Popular Paraphrase Versions of the Bible

The Message Bible (MSG)
The Living Bible (TLB)

THERE'S AN APP FOR THAT

In addition to your own hard copy Bible, you can obtain many of the translations and/or paraphrase versions of the Bible through various websites, apps or digital downloads that can be used on your digital readers. Check out these Bibles and tools.

Bible Apps and Digital Downloads

Bible!
YouVersion Bible
Olive Tree Bible Reader
Blue Letter Bible

Bible Study Tools Websites

www.biblestudytools.com
www.biblegateway.com
www.blueletterbible.org
www.biblos.com
www.ebible.com

To get started, I would recommend that you obtain a hard copy and/ or digital Bible right away. You might want to start with an easy to read translation. The New Living Translation (NLT) is a good choice for beginners because it's easy to understand.

As soon as you are ready to dig a little deeper, I would recommend you get additional translations of the Bible including: the New King James Version, the King James Version or the New International Version. When you want to go even deeper in the Word, I recommend you get the Amplified Bible and use some of the online Bible tools websites for great studies.

BUST THE DUST

It's great to have a Bible, but the secret for getting to know God, is to read it! There are a lot of Christians that need to "bust the dust" and start reading their Bibles again.

If you are new in the Lord, you might be unsure of where to start reading in the Bible. Of course, the entire Word of God is alive and powerful, but here are a few recommendations on where to begin reading.

As a rule, as a Christian you should spend most of your time reading the New Testament, since you are living under the New Covenant and these books were specifically written to Christians. However, reading the Old Testament is extremely beneficial and will give you a great historical overview. The Holy Spirit will speak to your heart as you read both the Old and New Testaments. Consider these thoughts:

> THE WORD OF GOD IS ALIVE AND POWERFUL.

The Old Testament: The Old Testament gives you the history of God's dealings with His people and His promises concerning the coming Messiah. In the Old Testament, the major divisions include: the Law, Historical, Poetry and Wisdom and Prophetic books. Through the Old Testament, you will see what it was like to live under the Law. This helps you understand the riches of God's mercy in the New Testament—under the New Covenant of Grace. God will reveal Himself to you as you read the Old Testament and will point you to the coming Messiah—Jesus.

The New Testament: The New Testament can generally be divided into these divisions: Gospels, History, Letters and Prophecy. The Gospels (Matthew, Mark, Luke and John) give you eyewitness accounts of Jesus—His life, ministry, death and resurrection. In the Gospels, you see Jesus preaching the good news everywhere as He fulfilled the Old

Testament Law, closed out the Old Covenant and ushered in the New Covenant.

History, Letters and Prophecy (Acts all the way to Revelation) make up most of the New Testament and these are written specifically to believers after Jesus died on the cross and was raised from the dead. The Letters give you the most detailed revelation concerning your redemption, the abundant life and what it means to be—*in Christ*. Revelation, the last book of the Bible, tells you about things to come.

READERS ARE LEADERS

It's true; readers are leaders! The more you read God's Word, the more wisdom He will give you. Being filled with God's wisdom will always make you a better Christian—and a great leader. There are many good reading plans that will help you read READ THE BIBLE. God's Word in a systematic way. Here are some recommendations on where to start reading in the Bible.

Start with the Gospel of John: One of the best books to start with is the Gospel of John. When you read the book of John, you will learn about Jesus, His life, ministry, love and truth. When you read the Gospel of John, you fall in love with Jesus.

Read Romans: The book of Romans can be a little deep, but if you are the type of person who trusted in your own good works before you became a Christian, the book of Romans will help you to get a comprehensive view of the gospel—God's goodness and free gift of salvation through grace and faith. When you read the Book of Romans, you will want to shout, "Thank You, Jesus!"

Read Psalms: The Psalms are in the Old Testament and are great heart-felt poems written by various Psalmists. It's easy to relate to the Psalms because many of them describe the cry of your own heart at times. When you read the Psalms, you will learn how to express your heart to the Lord in honest, heart-felt ways.

Read Proverbs: The book of Proverbs is in the Old Testament and it is loaded with practical, godly wisdom for life. You will obtain God's insight for almost every area of your life—knowing Him, relationships, work, school, marriage, parenting, money, words and so much more. When you read the book of Proverbs, your heart will be filled with the most important thing: wisdom!

Read Acts: The book of Acts is like reading an adventure-filled drama. You will be inspired by the boldness, influence—and persecution—of the Spirit-filled believers in the early church.

Read James: The book of James is a very practical book. In James, you will learn how to handle trials, how to live out your faith, how to control your tongue, how to pray and how to live a balanced Christian life.

Read Galatians, Ephesians, Philippians and Galatians: These four letters will fill you with insights and wisdom about your life *in Christ* and will help you live out your Christian life with joy, by faith.

Of course, the whole Bible is living and active—so no matter where you start reading you can count on the Lord to speak to your heart.

BELIEVE IT AND DO IT

God expects believers to believe Him! When we read His Word and hear Him talking to our hearts, He wants us to believe it. Faith pleases God.

On the other hand, be advised, your enemy doesn't want you to believe. One of his first tactics is to cast doubts on your faith. The devil wants to steal the Word before it can take root in your heart, so the best thing to do, even when you have doubts, is to keep reading the Word. His Word is alive, and as you allow the Lord to speak to your heart, He will answer your doubts with His living Word.

When you read something in the Bible, don't just believe it—do it! If you read a passage that tells you to seek God—believe it and then do it. If you read a pas-

GOD EXPECTS
BELIEVERS
TO BELIEVE.

sage that tells you to flee from sin or ungodly influences—believe it and then do it! If you read a passage that says God loves you and has forgiven you—believe it and then act like you believe it. If you don't know how to put God's Word into action, just ask Him. He will give you the wise insight you need to believe and do His Word.

Here's an example of the importance of believing God and doing His Word. In 1 John 1:9, it says, *"If we confess our sins, He is faithful and just to forgive our sins and cleanse us from all unrighteousness,"* and 2 Corinthians 5:21 says, *"For He made Him who knew no sin to be sin for us, that we might become the righteousness of God in Him."* (NKJV)

These passages are true. God wants you to believe them and act like you believe them. However, here's what can happen. Let's say you sin and feel guilty and full of shame. If you don't believe or do the Word, you will stay trapped in feelings of guilt and shame. God doesn't want you to live in a state of guilt, shame or unworthiness; He wants you to believe in His mercy, forgiveness and gift of righteousness.
Because of Jesus, your sins have already been forgiven and He has made you righteous. When you confess your sins, you will experience that forgiveness along with instant freedom from the guilt and shame.

Can you see that? The Lord wants you to believe that He has forgiven and cleansed you from all unrighteousness. He wants you to believe that He has made you the righteousness of God—as righteous as He Himself—because of Jesus. Then, He wants you to act like you believe it. If you will believe His Word, and act like a person who is forgiven and free from guilt and shame, you will experience great freedom, joy and gratitude!

DON'T LISTEN TO HATERS

One final word: don't let the haters lead you astray. Listen to this caution from the Bible, *"...I fear that somehow you will be led away from your pure and simple devotion to Christ,"* 2 Corinthians 11:3, NLT. There have always been, and will always be haters—people who hate, mock, dismiss, and ignore the Bible. There are some who want to rewrite or eliminate the Bible. The devil definitely hates the Word of God and the power it holds. He doesn't want any Christian to get, read, believe or do the Bible. Don't let the enemy or the negativity or ignorance of those who do not know God short-circuit your faith—get a Bible, read it, believe it, do it and watch God go to work in and through your life!

SCRIPTURES TO READ

___ Psalm 119
___ Luke 6:46-49
___ Luke 8:4-15
___ 1 Peter 1:24-25

STUDY GUIDE

Please review the previous chapter and use this Study Guide to journal the things you are learning about the Bible.

1. Do you have your own Bible? What version(s) do you have? List them all - hard copies, digital, apps, etc.

2. When you read the Bible, do you sense God speaking to your heart? Describe it:

3. What book(s) of the Bible are you reading right now?

4. What verse or passage of Scripture has hit home with you lately? What does it mean to you?

5. As you've read the Word, have you sensed the Holy Spirit asking you to start doing anything new? Has He asked you to stop doing some things? Describe:

BASIC #3
GET REAL IN PRAYER

Do you like to talk with people? How about texting? Connecting on Facebook, Twitter or the latest and greatest social media tool? How about meeting up for coffee with an old friend to catch up? There's something about heartfelt communication that helps us connect with others. The same is true in your relationship with the Lord.

God wants to connect with you! He wants you to get real in prayer.

HAVE A HEART TO HEART

Prayer is simply talking to the Lord from your heart. You don't have to make it more complex than it is. You don't have to be kneeling or lying face down to pray—although if you want to do so, that's fine—you just have to talk to the Lord from your heart.

When you pray, you are having an actual conversation with the Lord. You can picture it many ways. First, you could see yourself talking to the greatest President or King of all time and this would prompt you to be intentional, honoring and respectful in having strategic Kingdom conversations. Second, you could see yourself talking with your Heavenly Father and it will cause you to feel secure and loved as you pour out your heart or seek His insights. Third, you could see yourself talking with your dearest and wisest Friend to seek counsel or ask for whatever you need, knowing that He desires to help you and meet your needs. Fourth, you could see yourself talking with the highest ranking, military

Commander in Chief and this would cause you to be humble, submissive, excellent and attentive in your conversations. Get the idea? Our view of God should always be in line with His Word. We don't invent a God to pray to; we pray to the God we have encountered in the Word.

As you pray and talk to the Lord, you can ask questions and make requests for yourself, your family and friends and many others. You can pour out your cares, anxieties and thoughts to Him. You can ask for the impossible. You can request spiritual blessings, relational blessings, physical and material blessings. You can pray for people in high places, as well as those on the lowest rung. You can pray for rich and poor or young and old. You can pray for those who love you and those who are your sworn enemies. You can pray about everything and anything. You can pray about big things and little things. God is not too busy to hear your prayer requests—all shapes and sizes.

WHEN AND WHERE TO PRAY?

You can pray at anytime, anywhere! You can pray in your car, while going for a walk, on a bike, in bed, in the shower, on the treadmill, while playing golf or rocking your baby. You can pray when things are great or in crisis. You can pray while standing on your head, writing in a journal or swimming with dolphins. You can pray on a bus, in a plane or while at school. Really, you can talk to the Lord continuously. *"Evening and morning and at noon I will pray, and cry aloud, and He shall hear my voice,"* Psalm 55:17, NKJV.

> YOU CAN PRAY AT ANYTIME, ANYWHERE.

While you can pray at all times, it will help you to have a regular, daily quiet time—a time when you meet with the Lord to pray and read your Bible. Jesus talked about setting aside time to spend with God in our private place of prayer—a place where we could get alone with Him. *"But when you pray, go away by yourself, shut the door behind you, and pray to your Father in private. Then your Father, who sees everything, will reward you,"* Matthew 5:5, NLT.

As you get started in your walk with the Lord, what time of day would be best for you to meet with God? First thing in the morning? Late at night? Lunchtime? Pick a time and place and make that your special appointment with the Lord. To start, why not set aside 15 minutes a day to talk to the Lord about things that are on your mind and heart? As you do, God will fill you with wisdom and great joy, and the Lord will become very real and very personal to you.

WHAT SHOULD I PRAY ABOUT?

There are all kinds of things to pray about. Prayer is a time to thank God for what He has done. It's a time to praise and worship God for who He is. It's a time to cast your cares on the Lord. It's a time to hang out with the Lord and talk. Prayer is an opportunity to ask specific questions. It's a time to make special requests. It's a time to plead your case. It's a time to ask God for things on the behalf of others. Prayer is an experience of working with God to give your voice to the things that He puts on your heart. You can pray for the government, your family, missionaries, your neighbors, your church, yourself and many other things. There are so many fun dynamics to a real, comfortable prayer life. Let's look at some of the basics.

THE GOAL
IN PRAYER
IS TO CONNECT
WITH GOD.

HOW SHOULD I PRAY?

There are a lot of ways to pray. There isn't necessarily a right or wrong way to pray, but there are effective and ineffective ways to pray. Remember, God is a Person and we relate to Him just like we relate to people. Don't be stiff and don't be too loose or sloppy—remember, you are talking to the King of kings and Lord of lords. Prayer and talking to God is not like *clocking in* to a job—it's supposed to be a meaningful, enjoyable, heartfelt, rich, strategic time of personal interaction with the Lord—the One who loves you and whom you love. Jesus didn't like it when the people of His day prayed long, boring prayers for the ears of men—He rebuked them for being too mechanical in their approach to prayer. Listen to what He said, *"...when you pray, do not use vain repetitions as the heathen do. For they think they will be heard for their many words. Therefore do not be like them," Matthew 6:7-8, NKJV.*

The goal in prayer is to connect with God and to pray effective prayers. James 5:16 describes this type of prayer, *"...The earnest (heartfelt, continued) prayer of a righteous man makes tremendous power available [dynamic in its working]," AMP.*

When you pray, tap into your heart and let your prayers be earnest, heartfelt and constant. God will use your prayers to make tremendous power available for you and others!

BAM

To pray effective prayers, it helps to have a starting point. Let's look at a simple way to get started in prayer using the acronym: BAM!

Brag on God: Start your prayer time off by thanking God for what He has done for you. Brag on Him! Tell Him what you are thankful for. Then, take some time to praise and worship Him for who He is. As you spend time in the Word, you will get to know Him better and your heart will want to praise Him for being the Almighty Creator—loving, majestic, full of wisdom, favor, grace and goodness and so willing to be slow to anger and abundant in kindness, patience and generosity! See how easy it is to get started bragging on God?

THANK GOD FOR WHAT HE HAS DONE FOR YOU.

Follow the pattern in Psalm 100. *"On your feet now—applaud GOD! Bring a gift of laughter, sing yourselves into his presence. Know this: GOD is God, and God, GOD. He made us; we didn't make him. We're his people, his well-tended sheep. Enter with the password: 'Thank you!' Make yourselves at home, talking praise. Thank him. Worship him,"* Psalm 100:1-4, MSG.

Admit Your Dependence on God: God promises to bless the humble and reward those who have faith. *"And it is impossible to please God without faith. Anyone who wants to come to him must believe that God exists and that he rewards those who sincerely seek him,"* Hebrews 11:6, NKJV.

When you acknowledge your dependence upon Him, recognizing that you are the sheep and He is the shepherd, you open the door for God's blessings in your lives. If you approach God with an attitude of pride, arrogance or entitlement—God will resist you. The Bible says, *"God resists the proud, but gives grace to the humble,"* James 4:6, NKJV. If you are humble—He will give you honor. *"When you bow down before the Lord and admit your dependence on him, he will lift you up and give you honor,"* James 4:10, NLT.

Make Your Requests: Prayer is our vehicle for asking! There are many things the Lord could do and would do—if someone would just make a request and ask Him. For some reason, God wants us to ask. Although He knows everything, and can do anything, He has specifically installed *asking* and *believing* as the prerequisite for effective prayer. The Bible is full of exhortations for us to *ask* God for whatever we need.

"So I say to you, ask, and it will be given to you; seek, and you will find; knock, and it will be opened to you," Luke 11:9, NKJV.

"If you ask anything in My name, I will do it," John 14:14, NKJV.

"And whatever things you ask in prayer, believing, you will receive," Matthew 21:22, NKJV.

"Now this is the confidence that we have in Him, that if we ask anything according to His will, He hears us. And if we know that He hears us, whatever we ask, we know that we have the petitions that we have asked of Him." 1 John 5:14-15, NKJV.

Are you ready to start asking God for and about things? When you pray, believe! God likes it when we pray in faith, in accordance with His will as revealed in His Word. If you want to have an effective prayer life, always pray and make your requests in alignment with God's Word—in fact, it's good to pray God's Word! Make this your homework: look up these three prayers: Ephesians 1:15-23, Ephesians 3:14-20, Colossians 1:9-12 and then pray these for yourself and others by inserting your name and theirs into the prayer.

A MOST SATISFYING WAY TO PRAY

Finally, one of the most fulfilling and satisfying ways to pray is through singing! The Book of Psalms in the Bible is full of these kinds of prayers. When you sing

SING TO
THE LORD!

songs to and about God, you are praying! When you sing and thank or praise the Lord for what He has done for you and when you worship Him for who He is—you can't help but get filled with joy and hope!

The Bible tells us to *magnify* the Lord. When you magnify something— you make it bigger to you. When you magnify God—you don't actually make Him bigger—He is already as big as He is; you just make Him bigger to you. You may be going through a rough time, feeling discouraged, having doubts or feeling down, but when you put the magnifying glass on God and begin to sing about how great and magnificent He is—your troubles get very small and He gets very big in your life!

If you will get in the habit of singing to the Lord early in your Christian life, you will experience a very rich prayer life. You might not feel like a very good singer. Maybe you can't carry a tune to save your life. That's okay; the Lord likes it when we make a joyful noise to Him! *"Instead, be filled with the Holy Spirit, singing psalms and hymns and spiritual songs among yourselves, and making music to the Lord in your hearts. And give thanks for everything to God the Father in the name of our Lord Jesus Christ," Ephesians 5:18-20, NLT.*

You can sing to the Lord in a few different ways. One way is to simply sing a song from your heart to Him. In other words, you *make up* the song as you sing words that are in your heart. God loves this. The Bible is full of encouragement to sing a *new* song to the Lord. You can also sing old hymns or sing along with a playlist of praise and worship songs from Christian artists. So, go ahead—download some Jesus-exalting, faith-filled songs or grab a hymnal and belt out words of prayer and worship to the Lord.

7 WAYS TO PRAY

Pray for the authorities in your life. 1 Timothy 2:1-3
Pray in agreement with God's will. 1 John 5:14-15
Pray for wisdom. James 1:5
Pray by asking in Jesus' Name. John 14:13-14
Pray in the Spirit. Ephesians 6:18, Romans 8:26
Pray for Christian workers. Matthew 9:36-38
Pray by singing, thanking and praising God. Psalm 100

SCRIPTURES TO READ

___ Psalm 5
___ Matthew 6:5-13
___ Mark 11:23
___ John 14-16
___ Psalm 100, 150

STUDY GUIDE

Please review the previous chapter and use this Study Guide to journal the things you are learning about prayer.

1. Describe your prayer life. When and where do you like to meet with God for prayer?

2. What types of things are on your heart to pray about? List any specific people, questions or topics.

3. Using the BAM acronym for prayer, write out 2-3 sentences to just *Brag on God*.

4. Using the BAM acronym for prayer, write out 2-3 sentences to *Admit Your Dependence on God*?

5. Using the BAM acronym for prayer, *Make Your Requests* by writing down 2-3 specific things you're asking of God.

BASIC #4
GET INTO A GOOD CHURCH

You can be committed to church but not committed to Christ,
but you cannot be committed to Christ
and not committed to church.
Joel Osteen

You were not designed to do the Christian life all by your lonely self. God created you to have relationships with others. He wants you to be connected to people who will connect you to Him!

One of the main vehicles Jesus has established to strengthen, equip and encourage you in life, in relationships and in serving His purposes, is His Church. Jesus is building His Church and it is growing all over the world. We have found that those who are planted in a local church are some of the healthiest, most stable and fruitful Christians we know. Those who bounce all over and never quite get rooted into a local church seem to have a life that reflects instability and confusion. This is a huge piece of wisdom: get planted in a good church as soon as possible!

You might be fired up and full of zeal today, but if you don't get connected to a vibrant local church, your fire will slowly die. Being disconnected from the body of believers is like taking a log out of the big, raging bonfire and setting it off to the side. In time, the log that was glowing brightly will go out. God wants you to flourish, not flounder! It's no wonder the psalmist said this, *"Those who are planted in the house of the LORD shall flourish in the courts of our God,"* Psalm 92:13, NKJV.

FIND YOUR TRIBE

These days, people are definitely looking for a place to belong. They want to find their people, their tribe, their network, their gang and the group with whom they share common interests and passions. People want to work together with others to make a difference in this world—Jesus created us to be a part of His Church for these very reasons.

Sadly, some people have a bad taste in their mouth about church or organized religion. That's unfortunate, because Jesus has quite the opposite view. He loves His Church, warts and all! In fact, Jesus is called the Head of the Church. He has a very positive view of Church. He loves the Church so much; He is working from heaven to build His Church around the world.

Some people have been misled to think they don't need church. They figure they can stay home and watch a television evangelist or go for a walk in the woods and get just as close to God. Others feel they can get everything they need from God on their own—apart from church. There's only one problem. Jesus doesn't agree. Jesus is the one who called and established His church—and local church bodies—and He must have done so for a reason. Whether you're attending a church down the street or connecting with your church body through their online church service, the Bible is clear that *some assembly is required* if you want to grow into the healthy, balanced Christian God has called you to be. *"And let us not neglect our meeting together, as some people do, but encourage one another, especially now that the day of his return is drawing near," Hebrews 10:25, NLT.*

THERE IS NO SUCH THING AS THE PERFECT CHURCH. Some people think that because they believe the church is full of hypocrites, money hungry preachers or outdated, irrelevant, naive Christians, their AWOL (absent without leave) behavior is justified. Not sure they'll ever get God's approval on that. The reality is that there is no such thing as the perfect church. After all, the church is made up of imperfect people. That's life.

Think about it. Do you get a bad taste in your mouth about *organized football* because of a few hypocritical coaches who are on ego-trips? Do you quit going to hospitals forever because you had a physician who charged outrageous fees for an office visit? Do you get a bad attitude about hair salons because you had one stylist who was outdated, irrelevant, naive and gave you the worst haircut ever? Of course not, you just find another hospital, a different coach and a new salon.

Don't let the enemy to feed you his destructive lies about church. If you put your trust in people alone, you are bound to be disappointed, hurt, offended and disillusioned. If you keep your eyes on Jesus and make it a point to avoid being easily offended, you will flourish. When you run from the pitfalls of pride or being wise in your own eyes—

> DO YOURSELF A FAVOR, TRUST IN THE LORD.

common tactics the devil uses to split churches and divide people—you will do well. Do yourself a favor, trust in the Lord, honor those He has called to pastor your church and love your fellow Christians; then God will honor you by using that church to feed and lead you into a strong Christian life.

Don't allow the attitudes of a few negative people who have been offended or burnt by the Church—for whatever reason—dissuade you from getting plugged into a local church. Just remember, there is *always* more to the story—*always*. Before you believe negative things about any church, review the character and track record of that church and its leaders. Their history in the community should speak for itself. Jesus established the church for a reason and it's usually in your best interest to find out why and then agree with Him. While there is no perfect church, there are many God-honoring, Bible-preaching churches that are doing their best to follow Jesus and accomplish His will on earth. Pray and ask the Lord to help you find the church He has prepared for you.

THE HOUSE

Let's look at God's view of His church. There are several metaphors that help us understand the importance of church. Jesus called the gathering place of God's people, His House. Coming together with other believers is a powerful experience. His house should be a house of prayer, worship, Bible teaching and place where you can be encouraged, challenged, inspired, motivated, resourced, corrected and equipped in the Word.

Jesus is the Boss of His Church. He is the Head of His Body—the church. God's plan for leading and organizing His church is simple. He calls, anoints and equips specific individuals to serve as leaders in His church. They are responsible to plant, lead and feed local congregations of followers. These leaders are not to be self-appointed, but God-called and empowered.

Church leaders may have different titles depending on the church's culture. In a local church, the primary leader may be known as a: founder, senior pastor, lead pastor, shepherd, reverend, priest, apostle or bishop.

THE CHURCH IS SUPPOSED TO BE AN INTENTIONAL, GOD-APPOINTED, JESUS-LED, PURPOSE-DRIVEN, GATHERING OF GOD'S PEOPLE.

As a rule, the founding, senior or lead pastor is the one who is responsible before God for the leadership of the church. Often, as the church grows and reaches more people, the senior leader will delegate authority to other leaders in the church as the Lord guides and leads. These types of delegated leaders will include: executive pastors, associate pastors, Bible teachers, youth ministers, children's ministers, ministry directors, outreach or missions coordinators, worship or creative arts leaders, media tech directors, Sunday school teachers, team leads, support members, volunteer leaders and the like. God's church is not supposed to be a strife-filled, disorganized mess led by opinionated, self-appointed people hungry for power. It's supposed to be an intentional, God-appointed, Jesus-led, purpose-driven gathering of God's people.

THE METAPHORS

You can view church in many ways. The church can be compared to a flock, a family, a hospital, a gas station, a buffet, a team or an army. Let's take a look:

A Flock: The church is like a flock of sheep. The Bible tells us that Jesus is the Great Shepherd and we are His sheep. As sheep, we need a shepherd. It's not uncommon for sheep to get lost, or blindly follow other lost sheep right off a cliff. That's why God specifically calls individuals to be His shepherds (pastors)—to lead His flocks—(local churches). They are the shepherds of God's flock. These pastors are called, gifted and appointed by Jesus to lead, feed, train and equip Christians. Every Christian needs a shepherd/pastor and a flock/church where they can be cared for, fed and led.

Jesus described the difficult lot of people without a shepherd, *"When he saw the crowds, he had compassion on them because they were confused and helpless, like sheep without a shepherd,"* Matthew 9:36, NLT.

A Family: The church is like a family. God is your Father and He has given you *fathers, mothers, brothers and sisters* in the faith to help you grow up spiritually. They will love you, tell you the truth, pray with you, encourage you and serve you. They will be there for you in your time of need, as you will be there for them. A family is a safe place—a place where everyone can be himself or herself. In healthy families, everyone does their part to keep the home fires burning. Your church family is no different. Find a way to serve and become a contributing part of the family. Every Christian needs to be in a church that feels like home. The Bible calls God's family the *household of faith. "Therefore, as we have opportunity, let us do good to all, especially to those who are of the household of faith,"* Galatians 6:10, NKJV.

A Hospital: The church is like a hospital. There are times when we all need some first aid, rest, recovery and care. When you go through hard times, loss, challenges and afflictions—your church family will be there to comfort, pray and nurse you back to good spiritual health. This type of church is also a great place to bring those who are sick, hurting, unhealthy, and broken-hearted. It's so good to know that God is the Father of all comfort and He uses His

DON'T EVER FORGET, JESUS LOVES THE CHURCH.

Church to help comfort you in your time of need. *"All praise to God, the Father of our Lord Jesus Christ. God is our merciful Father and the source of all comfort. He comforts us in all our troubles so that we can comfort others. When they are troubled, we will be able to give them the same comfort God has given us,"* 2 Corinthians 1:3-4, NLT.

A Gas Station: The church is like a gas station. When you are living life, reaching out to others, facing battles and celebrating victories, your spiritual gas tank can get low. God wants your spiritual life to be on full and when you are attending, connected to and serving in a local church, the Lord will refill your tank with His Word and Spirit. I love the way the Message Bible tells us to stay full of God, *"Let's keep a firm grip on the promises that keep us going. He always keeps His word. Let's see how inventive we can be in encouraging love and helping out,* *not avoiding worshiping together as some do but spurring each other on, especially as we see the big Day approaching," Hebrews 10:25, MSG.*

A Buffet: The church is like a really nice buffet. You need to eat spiritual food on a regular basis. You need your meats, milk, vegetables, fruits as well as desserts. A healthy church provides a rich buffet of spiritual food so that men and women, boys and girls can pull up to the spread of God's Word and receive the nutrients they need to live a healthy and balanced Christian life. *"Your words were found, and I ate them, and Your word was to me the joy and rejoicing of my heart,"* Jeremiah 15:16, NKJV.

An Army: The church is like an army. God wants every believer to be armed and dangerous to the devil! He doesn't want anyone to eat so much at the spiritual buffet that they become a fat, slacker. That's why as soon as you became a Christian; the Lord enlisted you in His army!

GOD WANTS YOU TO BE ARMED AND DANGEROUS TO THE DEVIL!

The fact is, you are engaged in a very real spiritual battle. There is an enemy to your soul and he wants to steal, kill and destroy your life to make you ineffective. You need the discipline, training and development that comes from serving with God's troops. It's not always easy to be a Christian. It's rarely convenient. You will face temptations, trials, tribulations and challenges. You will be tempted to give up and quit. It takes discipline and soldier-like qualities to be a strong and effective Christian.

Your local church is a place where you can be trained, equipped and empowered to be a good soldier of Jesus Christ. You will learn how to use your spiritual weapons, keep rank, fight battles, quench fiery darts, win victories and thwart the enemy in your own life and on the behalf of others. *"You therefore must endure hardship as a good soldier of Jesus Christ. No one engaged in warfare entangles himself with the affairs of this life, that he may please him who enlisted him as a soldier,"* 2 Timothy 2:3-4, NKJV.

A Team: The church is like a team. It takes a lot of hard work, practice, rehearsals, discipline and the efforts of everyone on the team to accomplish kingdom wins! Jesus wants you and your church to win—to win in life and to win others to Christ. Every good team has a head coach and many players. Each person on the team makes a unique contribution based on his or her skill and talent. When God puts you in a local church, He wants you to wear that jersey and use your gifts to help that team play well. If you will follow the leadership of the head coach, be an unselfish team player and employ your talents for the good of the team, you will experience the joy and camaraderie of being on a winning team. The apostle Paul understood this, *"Then make me truly happy by agreeing wholeheartedly with each other, loving one another, and working together with one mind and purpose. Don't be selfish; don't try to impress others. Be humble, thinking of others as better than yourselves. Don't look out only for your own interests, but take an interest in others, too," Philippians 2:2-4, NLT.*

Can you see how wonderfully diverse the Church is? It's no wonder the devil hates the Church and tries to minimize, divide and destroy it. He will never be successful because Jesus loves and is building His Church! God has given us the incredible honor of being a part of the Church He loves. *Jesus said, "...upon this rock I will build my church; and the gates of hell shall not prevail against it," Matthew 16:18.*

JESUS IS BUILDING HIS CHURCH!

ABOUT PREFERENCES

Remember, no matter what church—flock, family, hospital, gas station, buffet, team or army—God plants you in, if you will remain humble and teachable—even after the initial novelty and "honeymoon" phase of finding a church home wears off—the Lord promises that you will flourish.

Don't ever forget, Jesus loves and is very serious about building His church. Do everything in your power to help Jesus *build* His church. Don't *tear* down His church by insisting on your own personal preferences—the programs you prefer, the color scheme you prefer, the songs or style of music you prefer, the attire you prefer or the service days and times you prefer. Being a part of God's church is not about your preferences; it's about His! Keep in mind, you won't be held responsible for the leadership of the church, your pastor will—so don't be the type of church person who complains, gossips, stirs up strife and causes grief when your preferences aren't met. Instead, be supportive and always bring a positive, unifying breath of fresh air to everyone around you.

7 QUESTIONS TO ASK WHEN LOOKING FOR A CHURCH

If you don't know what church to attend, ask around, go online and look for a church in your area. Here are seven questions to ask as you search for a Jesus-exalting, Bible-preaching, Spirit-filled church.

Does this church preach Jesus and exalt Him alone as the only Lord and Savior?

Does this church teach the Bible as the foundation and standard for faith?

Does this church feel alive and is the joy and power of the Holy Spirit evident in worship and the life of the church?

Does this church have effective, age-appropriate ministry for you and your kids or teens?

Does this church actively reach out to help lost, hurting and unchurched people?

Does the leadership of this church have good fruit in their own personal lives and does this church seem to be growing qualitatively and/or quantitatively?

Does this church offer opportunities to be trained, equipped or mentored, so you can grow in your faith and serve others?

Finally, when you add all of these things up—ask yourself if this church feels like *home* to you.

TAKE THE 12-WEEK CHALLENGE

Once you've found a church, take the 12-week challenge and attend that church every weekend for 12 weeks—about 3 months. My husband, Jeff, always encourages those who visit our church to take the 12-week challenge so they have a chance to get to know the church's vision, leaders, people and heart. Once you understand the culture of a church and meet some people, you will likely want to get more involved by serving, inviting others, becoming a part of a small group or taking classes.

JUMP IN WITH BOTH FEET. When you find a home church, make a decision to jump in with both feet! Don't sit on the sidelines. Don't become a critic. Don't be a freeloader. Get involved! When you become a participant instead of a spectator, the Lord can accelerate your spiritual growth. When you become a contributor and not just a consumer, the Lord will find multiplied ways to bless your life. When you *love, serve* and *give* in your local church, you will feel like an insider and not an outsider and you will open the door for God to do great things in and through you!

In closing, take a few moments to ponder these words about Jesus and His Church, *"...God raised Him from death and set Him on a throne in deep heaven, in charge of running the universe, everything from galaxies to governments, no name and no power exempt from His rule. And not just for the time being, but forever. He is in charge of it all, has the final word on everything. At the center of all this, Christ rules the Church. The Church, you see, is not peripheral to the world; the world is peripheral to the Church. The Church is Christ's body, in which He speaks and acts, by which He fills everything with His presence,"* Ephesians 1:20-23, MSG.

SCRIPTURES TO READ

___ Psalm 122:1
___ Psalm 133
___ Matthew 16:18
___ 1 Corinthians 12:28-29
___ Ephesians 4:7-15

STUDY GUIDE

Please review the previous chapter and use this Study Guide to journal the things you are learning about church.

1. Why do you think Jesus wants us planted in a church and not just doing the Christian life on our own?

2. Why is it important to understand God's calling, anointing and divine structure for a local church?

3. Of all the metaphors describing the church, which 3 impacted you the most? Why?

4. What is your understanding of the downside of preferences when it comes to being a vital part of a local church?

5. Do you have a home church? If so, great. If not, are you willing to take the *12-Week Challenge*? Reread the *7 Things to Look for in a Church* and write down one church you will attend for at least twelve weeks.

BASIC #5
GET EXCITED AND TELL SOMEBODY

No one has the right to hear the gospel twice,
while there remains someone who has not heard it once.
Oswald J. Smith

When exciting things happen in our lives, it's natural to want to tell everyone we know. When a girl gets engaged what does she want to do? When a young man buys a new car what does he want to do? They both want to tell everyone their good news! That's how you should feel about knowing Jesus.

Becoming a Christian is the best thing that has ever happened to you. Knowing Jesus and being completely forgiven of every sin you ever committed is definitely good news. It's better than winning the championship game, getting a new car, becoming engaged or finding a million dollars! Knowing Jesus is news worth shouting from the rooftops!

If you have been reluctant to share your faith, remember where you came from and look at how far God has brought you. Not too long ago, you were completely separated from God because of your sin. You had a one-way ticket to hell and your eternity was not looking too blissful. While you were still a sinner, God reached down with His love and mercy to touch your life. He worked in your heart for many months or years and drew you to Christ until the day you finally surrendered and confessed Jesus as your Lord.

At that moment, Jesus forgave all your sins, wiped your slate clean, pronounced you righteous and gave you a complete do-over. Not only that, He lives within your heart and He's promised to help you throughout the rest of your life. If that isn't enough, He's in heaven preparing a mansion for you so you can spend eternity with Him in a place where the streets are paved with gold. Now that's news worth sharing! You have been handpicked to walk with God Almighty—can you think of anything more compelling to tell the world?

HELP YOUR FAMILY AND FRIENDS GET IT

One of the best ways to stay filled with joy and to experience God's pleasure is by sharing your faith with others; one of the quickest ways to dry up on the vine is to keep your faith to yourself!

Don't forget, there are a lot of people who don't get it, yet. They don't get the God-stuff. They don't get Jesus or the Bible or church. They don't get why heaven and hell matter or why they should care about such things. They don't understand what's happened to you. Jesus needs genuine followers who will *go* into their world to help people get it—people who will share the gospel! If you are willing, God will use you to help others find Christ. Let's talk about it.

THERE ARE
A LOT OF PEOPLE
WHO DON'T GET IT, YET.

Have you wondered how to tell your family and friends about Jesus? Let's say you became a Christian today, now what? The church service is over, the conference has ended, the goose bumps have receded and it's time to go home to family members or friends who don't share your enthusiasm for the Lord.

What do you do when your spouse uses the Name of the Lord in vain or when your friends call you a goody two-shoes because you're not doing shots or getting high with them any longer? How do you respond when you're accused of being too naive or "holier than Thou"? How do you relate to family and friends who don't understand what Jesus has done in your life?

It's very possible that someone in your own family will mock you for *getting religious*. They might think you've dropped off the deep end or they might chalk up your enthusiasm for God as *a phase you're going through*. You will probably go to school or work with people who dismiss Christians, hate church, swear like a sailor and expect you to continue to party with them like there's no tomorrow. You might be misunderstood, teased and laughed at by people you love.

In a worst case, you will be rejected, scorned and slandered. The Bible tells us to expect some of these things, *"You have had enough in the past of the evil things that godless people enjoy—their immorality and lust, their feasting and drunkenness and wild parties, and their terrible worship of idols. Of course, your former friends are surprised when you no longer plunge into the flood of wild and destructive things they do. So they slander you. But remember that they will have to face God, who will judge everyone, both the living and the dead,"* 1 Peter 4:3-5, NLT.

So, what do you do? How should you relate to your family and friends in the first few days, weeks, months or years of becoming a Christian? What should you tell your spouse? Parents? Kids? Friends? Coworkers? Should you blow them out of the water by getting a megaphone and telling everyone they need to repent and get radically saved? Or should you hide in a closet or lie in the weeds for months on end and never tell a soul? Neither! You don't have to be the gospel police or a silent observer. Trust the Lord and He will show you how to effectively share your faith. Let's look at a few ways to be a light for Christ.

COME AND SEE

Initially, one of the best things you can do is to just *be* a Christian and let your light shine. The *come and see* approach is often the best way to get started in sharing your faith in Jesus with others. *"Let your light so shine before men, that they may see your good works and glorify your Father in heaven,"* Matthew 5:16, NKJV.

Let your walk with Jesus speak for itself. If you were a sarcastic, selfish person before Christ—when people hear kindness and see a new kind of unselfishness coming out of you—they will start asking you questions. If you were fearful and depressed before Jesus came into your life—when people see the light in your eyes and the joy in your voice—they will want to know what happened to you! If you were worldly, full of pride or self-ab-

LET YOUR WALK WITH JESUS SPEAK FOR ITSELF.

sorbed before Christ—when people see your humble heart and focus on others—they will know for sure that something good has happened to you and they will be all ears. Philip, one of Jesus' first followers, didn't try to hard sell Jesus to others, he simply walked with the Lord and said things like, *"Come and see..."* This approach is a good way to get started.

Peter, another disciple of Jesus, gave married people a good example of the *come and see* approach. He encouraged wives of unbelieving husbands to let their inner disposition shine, *"Be good wives to your husbands, responsive to their needs. There are husbands who, indifferent as they are to any words about God, will be captivated by your life of holy beauty. What matters is not your outer appearance—the styling of your hair, the jewelry you wear, the cut of your clothes—but your inner disposition. Cultivate inner beauty, the gentle, gracious kind that God delights in. The holy women of old were beautiful before God that way, and were good, loyal wives to their husbands,"* 1 Peter 3:1-6, MSG.

When your family and friends see the godly changes in your life, God will captivate their hearts. At times, sharing your faith with family and friends will bring you the greatest joy; at other times it may be your biggest challenge. Jesus experienced this Himself. When He went to His own hometown to preach the good news, everyone wasn't thrilled with Him. Many people who knew Jesus and His family were offended by His faith, while others received Him and His words.

Although there may be people in your life who don't get it, it's very likely that you have family and friends who are ripe and ready to hear about Jesus and they are longing for peace with God. When the time is right, God will help you know what to say and when to say it.

YOU HAVE GOOD NEWS!

When you sense the time is right to share the gospel with others here are few pointers.

YOU HAVE GOOD NEWS AND PEOPLE NEED IT!

You Have Good News: Never lose sight of the fact that you have good news and people need it! Many people are living in the constant state of bad news, darkness, fear, depression, rejection, anger, destruction and death. They need someone who has good news—someone with the light, faith, joy, acceptance, peace, restoration and life to enter their world. You are that someone!

You Are God's Method: God uses people to preach the good news. You are God's ambassador, *"Now then, we are ambassadors for Christ,* *as though God were pleading through us: we implore you on Christ's behalf, be reconciled to God," 2 Corinthians 5:20, NKJV.*

If God could preach the gospel without your help, He would. If Jesus could broadcast the good news from heaven's speaker system, He would. If angels could preach the gospel, they would. If God could drag people to church to hear the message, He would. The truth is God has commissioned you and me to be His messengers. Sharing the good news is our responsibility and joy. *"For 'Everyone who calls on the name of the LORD will be saved.' But how can they call on Him to save them unless they believe in Him? And how can they believe in Him if they have never heard about Him? And how can they hear about Him unless someone tells them? And how will anyone go and tell them without being sent? That is why the Scriptures say, 'How beautiful are the feet of messengers who bring good news!'" Romans 10:13-15, NLT.*

You Are Not Alone: Don't forget, you don't have to do this alone! Jesus promised to give you all the power and boldness you need to give our eyewitness account of knowing Him. When you go into the highways and byways of your sphere of influence; when you hit up office parties, college campuses, family reunions, business lunches or neighborhood play dates, ask the Holy Spirit to fill you with power to be a witness for Christ. Listen to what Jesus said, *"But you will receive power when the Holy Spirit comes upon you. And you will be My witnesses, telling people about Me everywhere—in Jerusalem, throughout Judea, in Samaria, and to the ends of the Earth," Acts 1:8, NLT.*

GO FISHING

Not only does Jesus call you His ambassador, messenger and witness, He calls you a fisherman. Have you ever gone fishing? There's nothing like getting up

IT'S FUN TO CATCH FISH!

early in the morning with a bucket of worms, fishing poles, a tackle box and a packed lunch. When we were growing up, my dad would take my three sisters and me fishing at Lake Missaukee in Michigan. We loved to fish for blue gills. We'd put a big worm on that hook, throw our fishing line into the water, and when the bobber went under the water, we pulled up on that pole and *snapped their eyes out*. We never complained about going fishing; it was fun to catch fish!

In the same way, being a *fisher of men* for Christ should be fun, exciting and exhilarating, not something you fear, despise or do out of duty. If you follow Jesus, He'll show you how to fish. He'll guide you in what "bait and lure" to use in order to hook people with God's love.

To get started, here are a few helpful hints.

7 WAYS TO FISH FOR MEN

Pray for fish—ask God to help you reach lost people.

Use the right bait—listen to people share their hearts and they will tell you what type of bait to use.

Put your hook in the water—invite people to come to church.

Cast a wide net—host a big party and invite unchurched people.

Use a fish finder—find out what people need and meet it.

Throw some chum in the water—give people something to read or listen to: good Christian books, CDs, web links, videos and relevant Christian music.

Wait for the bobber to go down—when people open up about pain and challenges they are facing, offer to pray for them and introduce them to the God that loves them.

WHAT NOT TO DO

When it comes to getting excited and sharing your faith, let's talk about what not to do.

First: Don't keep the good news to yourself! The Dead Sea is a good example of what not to do. Water from the Jordan River flows into the Dead Sea, but there is no outflow from the Dead Sea. The result of receiving, but not giving, is to become dead! Be the type of Christian that receives a daily inflow of God's presence in your life and then share Him with others so you don't become like the Dead Sea. Don't let selfishness or the fear of man paralyze you; instead, be the type of person who is always looking for ways to share your faith and the goodness of God with others.

Second: Don't preach the bad news! Remember, Jesus called you to preach the good news. Sometimes, Christians mean well but they come across so negative, judgmental and critical. If you are condescending, or self-righteous, people will pick up on that right away and they will tune out. Be careful about sharing your faith with what can be perceived as a mean-spirit and phrases like, *"You're a sinner and going to hell..."* This definitely sounds like bad news! While it may be true, if you start off by sharing the bad news, you may have a hard time getting people to listen long enough to hear the good news. Try sharing the good news first, *"God loves you and Jesus came to give you an abundant life. And...."*

When you share the news about a God who loves them, they may open their hearts long enough to hear about Jesus and the reality of heaven and hell. Remember, the good news is John 3:16, *"God so loved the world that He gave is only begotten Son that whoever believes in Him would not perish, but have everlasting life."* If you would like a great little tool for sharing the good news of gospel with others, I highly recommend *The Four Spiritual Laws* booklet or app by Bill Bright.

Third: Don't be obnoxious or hyper-spiritual. You don't have to put on some type of freaky personality or a hellfire and brimstone dialect to share the good news of Jesus. Just be yourself and talk with others in your normal manner of communicating. Be compassionate, caring, bold and loving as you share the joy you have in knowing Jesus.

SCRIPTURES TO READ

___ John 3
___ Luke 15
___ Matthew 9:36-38
___ 1 Corinthians 9:19-22

STUDY GUIDE

Please review the previous chapter and use this Study Guide to journal the things you are learning about sharing your faith.

1. What makes Jesus and the gospel such good news?

2. Write down the names of 5 people you know who don't *get it*. Commit to pray for these five people for the next 60 days. Pray that God will open their hearts to the gospel.

3. What do you think will be the biggest challenge or obstacle for you to overcome to get excited and comfortable in sharing your faith in Jesus with others?

4. If someone said, "Tell me about Jesus and how to be saved," what would you tell them? Make a list of 5 Scriptures you would share with them and write down the salvation prayer you would share with them.

5. Write down the name of the top 2 people you are going to go fishing for. What type of bait, lures, chum and fishing tools is the Lord leading you to use to help *catch* them for Christ?

BASIC #6
GET YOUR HEAD ON STRAIGHT

We choose what attitudes we have right now.
And it's a continuing choice.
John C. Maxwell

How is your Christian life going? Are you enjoying getting to know the Lord? Are you still experiencing the joy of your salvation? Do you have questions? Have you made a few mistakes and wondered if the Lord was mad at you? Are you struggling with some old thought patterns and trying to figure out what to do with them?

No matter what you are facing right now, be encouraged in knowing that God wants to help you get the victory! The process of growth in our lives is called: *sanctification*. Day by day God sanctifies us—sets us apart and makes us more and more like Jesus. If you've been struggling, don't be discouraged. God will help you. He wants your life to be a progressive experience of one triumph after another. *"In the Messiah, in Christ, God leads us from place to place in one perpetual victory parade,"* 2 Corinthians 2:14, MSG. After all, Jesus said, *"...I came that they may have and enjoy life, and have it in abundance (to the full, till it overflows),"* John 10:10, AMP. To enjoy this perpetual victory and the abundant life, you will have to trust the Lord and His Word and get your head on straight.

As a Christian who is serious about walking with the Lord, you can be disconcerted and frustrated when you mess up or when bad, ungodly thoughts enter your mind. Before you became a believer in Jesus, you probably had some *stinkin' thinkin'*—but you may not have noticed all the negative thoughts that assaulted your mind. They may have seemed *normal* for you. However, as you grow in the Lord, you will become aware of the thoughts and behaviors that work against you. As you read the Bible and get closer to God, you will want to get rid of the ungodly ways of thinking and behaving that you've been accustomed to. So, to help you overcome whatever battles you may face, let's unpack some basic truths on what God says about you!

YOU ARE A THREE-PART PERSON

YOU ARE A SPIRIT. YOU HAVE A SOUL. YOU LIVE IN A BODY. You might not know this, but you are a three part being! You are a spirit, you have a soul and you live in a body. God wants to work in all three parts of your being. *"Now may the God of peace make you holy in every way, and may your whole spirit and soul and body be kept blameless until our Lord Jesus Christ comes again," 1 Thessalonians 5:23, NKJV.* When you understand how God has wired you, you will be able to focus your attention in the right place. Let's look at who you are in the light of God's Word to see if we can better understand His progressive work in your life.

You Are a Spirit: You are a spirit being. Your spirit (also called your heart) is the real you. It's the core of you. The person who lives behind your eyeballs is the real you—the spirit man. Your spirit is also called the *hidden man of the heart,* or the *inner man.* You are a spirit and God is the Father of spirits. When you confessed Jesus as your Lord and became a Christian, your spirit was instantly born again and changed. You are forgiven, made righteous and have become an entirely new person. The real you is a new person—a new creation in Christ! Your old spirit or heart has been removed and the Lord has given you a new spirit or heart. *"I will give you a new heart and put a new spirit within you; I will take the heart of stone out of your flesh and give you a heart of flesh," Ezekiel 36:26, NKJV.*

You Have a Soul: Your soul consists of your mind, emotions and will. Your soul is your personality; it is distinct from your spirit. Most of the battles you face will be struggles in your soul. With God's help you can learn the secrets of getting victory in your thoughts, emotions and choices.

As we've already seen, when Jesus became the Lord of your life, He forgave all your sins and He gave you a new spirit or heart. This gives you a tremendous feeling of freedom and peace in your spirit. However, you may have noticed that at times, your soul—mind, emotions and choices—still feel sinful and guilty. You may still be caught in mental, emotional or willful patterns of addictive behavior, fear, anxiety, depression, lust, jealousy, bitterness, anger or defeat. You may feel like an internal battle is going on between what you know to do in your spirit (heart) and what your soul (mind, emotions or will) wants to do. The Lord doesn't want you to stay in a place of internal conflict. He wants you to experience the same lasting freedom in your soul that you are experiencing in your spirit.

Look at this passage in Romans; does this battle of the soul sound familiar? *"I don't really understand myself, for I want to do what is right, but I don't do it. Instead, I do what I hate. But if I know that what I am doing is wrong, this shows that I agree that the law is good. So I am not the one doing wrong; it is sin living in me that does it. And I know that nothing good lives in me, that is, in my sinful nature. I want to do what is right, but I can't. I want to do what is good, but I don't. I don't want to do what is wrong, but I do it anyway. But if I do what I don't want to do, I am not really the one doing wrong; it is sin living in me that does it. I have discovered this principle of life—that when I want to do what is right, I inevitably do what is wrong. I love God's law with all my heart. But there is another power within me that is at war with my mind. This power makes me a slave to the sin that is still within me. Oh, what a miserable person I am! Who will free me from this life that is dominated by sin and death? Thank God! The answer is in Jesus Christ our Lord,"* Romans 7:15-25, NLT. Thankfully by faith, you can echo the Apostle Paul, "Thank God, Jesus is still helping me today!"

You Live in a Body: Your physical body is the house you—your spirit and soul—live in while you are on earth. You are not your body; your body carries your spirit and soul while you are alive on earth. It's your earthly costume. Your body is the vehicle God gave you to travel in while you are on earth. When you became a Christian, your body didn't change too much. Did you notice that? If you had blue eyes, were overweight or wore size 10 shoes before you got saved— you still have blue eyes, are overweight and wear size 10 shoes the day after you became a Christian.

YOU ARE NOT YOUR BODY.

When your body dies and you breathe your last breath, you (the real you—your spirit) will leave your physical body and go to be with the

Lord. So, what role does your body play in your Christian life? The Bible says your body is His temple. *"Or do you not know that your body is the temple of the Holy Spirit who is in you, Whom you have from God, and you are not your own,"* 1 Corinthians 6:19, NKJV.

Since your body is the Lord's temple, He wants to help you control your body. As you may already know, your body wants to be in charge of things. Your appetites and lusts want to call the shots and dominate your life. It's no wonder so many people get caught up in obsessive disorders and addictions to food, drugs, alcohol and pornography. The body screams for these things. However, if you will present your body as a living sacrifice to the Lord, and renew your mind with God's Word—He will work in your life and help you control your body.

Not only does God wants to help you control your body; He wants to use you and your body for His purposes. To do that fully, He also desires you to be strong, healthy and well. *"Beloved, I pray that you may prosper in all things and be in health, just as your soul prospers,"* 3 John 2, NKJV. You may need the Lord's overhaul in your body. If your body is weak or if you've abused your body, the Lord can bring restoration over time. As you walk with Him, your strength will be renewed and your countenance will start to glow. Your eyes will light up and your smile will come more easily. Your body can experience renewed health, wellness, energy and strength—especially as you listen to the Lord's promptings as it relates to the care of your spirit, soul and body.

THE BATTLEFIELD OF THE MIND

This all sounds great on paper, right? You are a spirit, you have a soul and you live in a body—and God wants to lead you in a perpetual victory parade! The question is, how does this work in real life?

THE BIGGEST BATTLE MOST CHRISTIANS FACE IS THE BATTLEFIELD OF THE MIND.

It starts with your thinking. Let's zoom in on our soul—specifically our thought life. Right thinking leads to right believing and right believing leads to right actions and right actions lead to a transformed life.

The biggest battle most Christians face is the battlefield of the mind. What does this battlefield look like? It sounds something like this: You are going along fine—living your Christian life and loving God. One day, you start to have thoughts that bother you: tempting thoughts, ungodly thoughts and impure thoughts. In a moment of weakness, you make a mistake and sin. You feel bad. Guilt plagues you. Now, you picture God as being angry and upset with you; you believe you deserve to feel guilty and probably punished in some way. New thoughts of shame and negativity enter your mind. You begin to think you are a real screw up. You can't do anything right. God will probably stop blessing your life. He'll close the door and you won't get the job you want. Or, God will probably tell your girlfriend to break up with you; or He will punish you by making your baby get sick or He'll cause you to have a car accident. After all, you deserve it and God probably wants to really teach you a lesson. The next thing you know, your thoughts have created a stronghold in your life and you're running from this monster you call God—rather than running to your loving Father God to experience His mercy and forgiveness!

If you don't know what to do with your thoughts, you will imagine all kinds of things that are not true. Can you see how quickly this type of wrong thinking discourages new Christians? Be wise and advised—your biggest spiritual battles will be between your ears—in your mind! When you recognize the source of negative, ungodly, tempting thoughts, and when you know what to do with them, you will be well on your way to living in perpetual victory.

> IF YOU DON'T KNOW WHAT TO DO WITH YOUR THOUGHTS YOU WILL IMAGINE ALL KINDS OF THINGS THAT ARE NOT TRUE.

Where do the thoughts that you battle come from? Your enemies! Let's look at three enemies every Christian faces.

THREE ENEMIES

There are three enemies that you must face. These three enemies often overlap and can be summarized as: the devil, the world and your fallen flesh. Once you identify the source of your battles, the Lord can help you defeat them. Let's take a look.

Enemy #1: The devil! You have an adversary—the devil, Satan, Lucifer, the deceiver—comes against you with lies and deceptive thoughts to sidetrack you from walking with the Lord. As soon as you decided to follow Jesus, you became a target. You have an enemy to your faith.

When you were blind and living large in the kingdom of darkness, the enemy didn't care about you. However, as soon as you declared Jesus as the Lord of your life, the devil put you on his hit list.

Don't let that rattle you. Your adversary has been completely defeated! Jesus absolutely conquered the devil and destroyed, disarmed and defanged our foe! Through His life, ministry, death on the cross and resurrection, Jesus triumphed over the devil and crushed him. The devil does not have any legitimate weapons, so he must resort to using lies and deception to snare and devour God's people. The devil's primary strategy is deception. In fact, the devil couldn't tell the truth if he wanted to because he is the father of lies.

THE DEVIL DOESN'T WANT YOU TO WALK WITH JESUS. The devil doesn't want you to walk with Jesus or to experience victory, so he will try to deceive you into a life of defeat by sending thoughts of temptation, pride, guilt, shame, doubt, defeat, fear, jealousy, envy, bitterness, resentment, selfishness, immorality and evil things to work against your mind. To snuff out these lies and deceptive thoughts, stay submitted to God and His Word. Resist the devil and he will flee. *"Therefore submit to God. Resist the devil and he will flee from you. Draw near to God and He will draw near to you,"* James 4:7-8, NKJV.

Enemy #2: The temptations of the world! God made this world to be a beautiful place loaded with His blessings. All of Creation reveals God's fingerprints; we should be grateful as we enjoy the blessings God has given to us. However, this world is also a fallen place and full of ungodly, evil, illegal, immoral, perverse and unethical attitudes, agendas and options. The Lord tells us to be aware of this temptation, *"Don't copy the behavior and customs of this world, but let God transform you into a new person by changing the way you think. Then you will learn to know God's will for you, which is good and pleasing and perfect,"* Romans 12:2, NLT.

The world is always trying to lure you into its behavior, customs and ways of thinking. By God's definition, the world includes: the lust of the flesh, the lust of the eyes and the pride of life. *"Do not love the world or the things in the world. If anyone loves the world, the love of the Father is not in him. For all that is in the world—the lust of the flesh, the lust of*

the eyes, and the pride of life—is not of the Father but is of the world,"
1 John 2:15-17, NKJV.

How does a Christian resist the thoughts of worldliness that plague him or her everyday? How does a Christian love people in the world, but not love the world? How does a Christian live in the world, but not become seduced by the temptations of the world? Let's examine how God wants to help us deal with: the lust of the flesh, the lust of the eyes and the pride of life.

The Lust of the Flesh: The lust of the flesh is all around us. It is often described as unlawful or forbidden sexual desires and can include anything else our flesh wants to consume in an excessive way—things not permitted by God. The lust of the flesh includes things like the inordinate love and obsessive desire for food, alcohol, partying, drugs, sex outside of marriage, pornography, money or material things. The lust of the flesh can include other things, like: jealousy, envy, rage, anger, fighting, strife and idolizing or worshipping people or things other than God.

The Lust of the Eyes: The lust of eyes is the unhealthy longing, craving, desire for what is forbidden. These days our eyes see all kinds of forbidden fruit. Just turn on the TV and you'll see a host of lifestyles, products or positions people lust after. Our eyes are never satisfied and we always see things we want. If we aren't careful the lust of the eyes through impurity, materialism, greed, indulgence and selfishness will dominate our lives and crowd out God.

The Pride of Life: The pride of life is the empty, presumptuous talk of braggarts. Pride causes us to trust in our status, resources, ego and power and leads us to despise humility and trusting in God. The pride of life is subtle, but easily leads to narcissistic behavior and the worship of self—over and above the worship of God.

The key to progressively overcoming the world—the lust of the flesh, the lust of the eyes, the pride of life—is to draw near to Jesus and make good choices. You don't have to yield to these temptations;

DRAW NEAR
TO JESUS
AND MAKE
GOOD CHOICES.

instead, if you will guard the gates on your ears and eyes—God will help you. How's this for a way to live? *"I will be careful to live a blame-*

less life—when will you come to help me? I will lead a life of integrity in my own home. I will refuse to look at anything vile and vulgar. I hate all who deal crookedly; I will have nothing to do with them. I will reject perverse ideas and stay away from every evil. I will not tolerate people who slander their neighbors. I will not endure conceit and pride. I will search for faithful people to be my companions," Psalm 101:2-6, NLT.

Enemy #3: Our fallen flesh. No matter how you slice it, even though Jesus is the Lord of your heart and spirit, you still have flesh—a body, a mind, a will and emotions that are very experienced at sinning. Your fallen flesh has a tendency to want to do what it has always done—sin and get its own way.

Have you noticed that your flesh has a loud voice? It screams, has temper tantrums, pity parties and makes all kinds of noise to get its own way! This is what creates an internal battle for you. In your heart, you know what you should do, but your flesh doesn't like to obey God; it wants to be in charge. To win the battle and overcome the desires of your fallen flesh, you're going to have to let the Spirit guide you as you keep growing spiritually. It's a process.

LET THE
HOLY SPIRIT
GUIDE YOUR LIFE.

The Bible says, *"So I say, let the Holy Spirit guide your lives. Then you won't be doing what your sinful nature craves. The sinful nature wants to do evil, which is just the opposite of what the Spirit wants. And the Spirit gives us desires that are the opposite of what the sinful nature desires. These two forces are constantly fighting each other, so you are not free to carry out your good intentions. But when you are directed by the Spirit, you are not under obligation to the law of Moses. When you follow the desires of your sinful nature, the results are very clear: sexual immorality, impurity, lustful pleasures, idolatry, sorcery, hostility, quarreling, jealousy, outbursts of anger, selfish ambition, dissension, division, envy, drunkenness, wild parties, and other sins like these. Let me tell you again, as I have before, that anyone living that sort of life will not inherit the Kingdom of God. But the Holy Spirit produces this kind of fruit in our lives: love, joy, peace, patience, kindness, goodness, faithfulness, gentleness, and self-control. There is no law against these things! Those who belong to Christ Jesus have nailed the passions and desires of their sinful nature to His cross and crucified them there. Since we are living by the Spirit, let us follow the Spirit's leading in every part of our lives," Galatians 5:16-25, NLT.*

Do you see more clearly how the battlefield of the mind works? Remember, Jesus has defeated all of your enemies and has given you all the tools you need to win the battle. Let's drill down and get even more practical.

HOW TO GET YOUR HEAD ON STRAIGHT

As you can see, one of the most important things you will ever learn in the Christian life is how to get your head on straight. When you develop the habit of renovating your thoughts, your life will be transformed. That's exactly what Romans tells us, *"And do not be conformed to this world, but be transformed by the renewing of your mind, that you may prove what is that good and acceptable and perfect will of God," Romans 12:2, NKJV.*

In order to experience lasting transformation in various areas of your life, you must renew your mind. You must think new thoughts! If you will take time to reprogram your mind —literally, renovate your mind— with God's truth, your old thoughts will be replaced with His thoughts. When you read and meditate on God's Word, His thoughts will replace your thoughts. That internal battle you sometimes experience

BE TRANSFORMED BY RENOVATING YOUR MIND.

will be less and less frequent and your spirit, soul and body will be more congruent and harmonious with God and His will for your life. Can you see it? When you allow the Word of God to saturate your mind, you will be transformed!

Let's take a final look at how this process works so you can get the victory in your thought life. This is the general process of a negative thought:

Bad Thoughts: First, negative or destructive thoughts come to your mind. *"Hey, you're lonely and sad. No one likes you. Your life stinks. Your marriage is empty. You don't have any fun. Your so-called Christian life is boring and pitiful. You'll always be a failure. You should just quit this whole Christian thing."* These thoughts percolate in your mind and if they are not taken captive, they go to the second level.

Bad Arguments: At the second level, those thoughts become an argument or presumption. You find yourself arguing to defend the thoughts that came to your mind. *"I deserve better! Just think about how much fun I could have at that wild party! Being faithful to my spouse is over-rated; one more fling won't hurt anything. Pornography isn't that bad, I deserve a little pleasure. I can smoke one joint. I need to drown my sorrows and get wasted. These Christians are losers; who says I need all this Jesus, Bible, church stuff? I'm just going to go back to my old life. Those are my real friends...."* You begin to imagine yourself fulfilling that thought.

Bad Strongholds: Third, if you don't do something about these thoughts, arguments, presumptions or imaginations they will become a stronghold in your life and you will be transformed into doing these very things. You'll act on those thoughts and before you know it, you will find yourself trapped in a lifestyle you don't want. Strongholds will have a grip on you. You will do the very things you want to be set free from.

This whole process started with your thoughts. Can you see the importance of getting your head on straight by thinking the right thoughts? The thought process we have outlined is found in the Bible, *"For though we walk in the flesh, we do not war according to the flesh. For the weapons of our warfare are not carnal but mighty in God for pulling down strongholds, casting down arguments and every high thing that exalts itself against the knowledge of God, bringing every thought into captivity to the obedience of Christ,"* 2 Corinthians 10:3-5, NKJV.

Let's look at this same process in a positive light. We can experience the godly transformation we desire if we choose to renew our minds with God's good thoughts. Let's look at how to develop *healthy strongholds*:

GET YOUR HEAD ON STRAIGHT BY THINKING THE RIGHT THOUGHTS.

Good Thoughts: First, those same ungodly, discouraging thoughts come to you. *"Hey, you're lonely and sad. No one likes you. Your life stinks. Your marriage is empty. You don't have any fun. Your so-called Christian life is boring and piti-ful. You'll always be a failure. You should just quit this whole Christian thing."* Instead of agreeing with these thoughts, your job is to take those thoughts as captives to Jesus, *"Jesus, what do you think about these thoughts? I give them to You. Even though I feel discouraged and* alone, I believe You and Your Word. I know You love me and You will bring good friends into my life. I know You have a good plan for my marriage. I know You want the best for my life. Help me to be strong today."

Good Arguments: Second, you begin to argue for these things. "Jesus, with my eye of faith I see that You are with me. Your finished work on the cross paid the price for me to experience a perpetual victory. I can picture You giving me favor with people and leading me to new friends and opportunities. I can see You helping my spouse and I fall in love again. I am content and at peace because I have You and I know You are filling my life good things. I have no plans to quit. I love my life with You."

> THIS ISN'T A MAGIC BULLET. BY FAITH, YOU WILL HAVE TO FIGHT FOR THESE THOUGHTS.

Good Strongholds: Third, you will have to intentionally think these thoughts moment-by-moment, day-after-day for a period of time until they are so ingrained in your mind and heart they literally become a healthy stronghold. Once this stronghold is built in your thought life, you will begin to experience the fruit of those thoughts. A life of expectation, provision, joy, peace, freedom, contentment, fulfillment, satisfaction, strength and victory will become the norm for you.

These are simplistic examples. In your life, things may not feel so simple! To get the victory God wants for you, you may have to be very intentional about putting these things into practice to overcome strongholds of failure, rejection, depression, self-pity, laziness or addictions that run your life. This isn't a magic bullet. By faith, you will have to fight for these good thoughts, arguments, imaginations and strongholds. Be consistent and be patient.

WE ARE ALL A WORK IN PROGRESS

Don't be discouraged if you are not where you want to be. You'll get there! We are all a work in progress and at various stages of our own spiritual growth and maturity. While several miraculous things happened the moment you got saved; there are numerous other things that the Lord will progressively transform throughout your entire life. Becoming a Christian and being a Christian are both an instantaneous event and a progressive process. As you take these things to heart and get control of your thoughts, you will experience consistent victory in your life.

7 THINGS TO THINK ABOUT

God doesn't need you to invent thoughts; He just needs you to believe His thoughts! The Bible tells us what kinds of thoughts to think, use this as an outline for getting your head on straight. *"Finally, brethren, whatever things are true, whatever things are noble, whatever things are just, whatever things are pure, whatever things are lovely, whatever things are of good report, if there is any virtue and if there is anything praiseworthy—meditate on these things," Philippians 4:8, NKJV.*

Remind yourself of these seven things every day.

True things: You are born again. You have passed from death to life. (John 3:6, 5:24)

Noble things: You are righteous. You are acquitted of all sin and made as righteous as God. (2 Corinthians 5:21)

Just things: You were transferred from the kingdom of darkness into the kingdom of God's Son. (Colossians 1:13)

Pure things: You have been adopted as God's child and welcomed to His family. (Romans 8:15)

Lovely things: You were recreated into a brand new person; the old is gone and the new has come. (2 Corinthians 5:17)

A report of good things: You were placed "in Christ" and God sees you "in Him"—found, forgiven and favored! (Ephesians 1:6-7)

Virtuous and praiseworthy things: Your name is written in God's Book of Life and recorded in heaven's Guest List. (Revelation 20:11-15)

SCRIPTURES TO READ

___ Romans 8
___ Psalm 23
___ Philippians 2
___ 2 Corinthians 10
___ Galatians 5

STUDY GUIDE

Please review the previous chapter and use this Study Guide to journal the things you are learning about getting your head on straight.

1. In your own words, describe your understanding being a three-part being: spirit, soul and body.

2. What three enemies work against you?

3. According to Romans 12:2, you can be transformed by renewing/renovating your mind. What does this look like for you?

4. What is the process for establishing good strongholds in your life?

5. List seven specific things God wants you to think about.

BASIC #7
GET READY FOR THE ADVENTURE

I just want to do God's will.
And he's allowed me to go to the mountain.
And I've looked over, and I've seen the promised land!
Martin Luther King, Jr.

There is nothing like the adventure of the Christian life! God has a divine purpose for you to fulfill. You are not some random, unimportant person just stumbling through life; you're a person of destiny with all kinds of God-given potential! You've been marked by God—chosen by Him—to live a life of significance. If you will follow Jesus and live out the faith-adventure He has for you; His fingerprints of goodness, blessing and favor will show up all over your life!

No matter what paths the Lord leads you to take, with God the Father on your side, with Jesus and the power of His Name given to you and with the great Holy Spirit living within you, you will always have the supernatural edge! If all of that isn't enough, He has given you His living Word to guide you and His wisdom, strength, grace and power to navigate every road and overcome every obstacle. You are poised for a great adventure!

THIS IS A FAITH ADVENTURE

The Christian life *is* a faith adventure! It's a life of believing God and believing His Word. It's a life of seeing the invisible and doing the impossible.

The faith life is the most exciting—and sometimes the most challenging—life there is. Faith enables you to face anything, overcome all things, and receive everything. God has called us to live by faith. Faith is like oxygen for the Christian. It's what you breathe! You believe God. You believe His Word. You know that with God all things are possible! God likes faith! Faith pleases Him. In fact, *"...without faith it is impossible to please Him, for he who comes to God must believe that He is, and that He is a rewarder of those who diligently seek Him," Hebrews 11:6, NKJV.*

Faith is simply taking God at His Word. He said it. You believe it. Faith is not found in your five physical senses. Faith is not a feeling. As believers, *"...we walk by faith, not by sight," 2 Corinthians 5:7, NKJV.* Faith comes from hearing God's Word. As you grow in the Word, you will grow in faith. You will experience the joy of hearing God speak to your heart and seeing His promises come alive. No matter what you face in life, as you take God at His Word, you will see He is faithful to fulfill His promises. *"God is not human, that he should lie, not a human being, that he should change his mind. Does he speak and then not act? Does he promise and not fulfill?" Numbers 23:19, NIV.*

WE WALK BY FAITH, NOT BY SIGHT.

Sometimes, when you live out the Christian adventure, you will have to fight the good fight of faith! In other words, some days, you may feel like you're full of faith and on top of the world and at other times it will seem as if the whole world is against you. Sometimes, you'll feel like the Lord has blessed you beyond belief and at other times, it will seem as though He has not heard your prayers. Some days you'll feel like you could tackle anything you face and other days you'll be tempted to quit. Don't pay too much attention to your feelings; instead fight the good fight of faith by believing God and His Word—no matter what! Stay strong in the Lord and steady in your faith.

The best way to stay full of faith is to feed on God's Word. Reading the Bible will fuel your faith and help you live a life pleasing to God. Are you getting stirred up to live out the faith adventure? I hope so!

YOU HAVE A SUPERNATURAL GUIDE

You don't have to walk out the faith-filled, Christian adventure all by yourself. You have a supernatural guide—the Holy Spirit—and He lives in you! We've talked about the Spirit before, but this is a good time to be reminded of His role in your life. You need the power of the Holy

Spirit and He wants to help you. He knows every route your life will take. He will help you navigate around narrow passages, up steep climbs, through long deserts and into flowing rivers.

As you follow His Word and the promptings of His still small voice, He will guide you in all the affairs of life. Not only will the Holy Spirit guide you from *within*; He wants to come *upon* you and fill your life to overflowing. If you will ask and yield to the Holy Spirit, He will grant you His supernatural ability to live out the Christian adventure. That means He will empower your life with these kinds of things: power to live for Christ, revelation to understand the Word; maturity to produce fruit; wisdom to experience the gifts of the Spirit; boldness to talk about Christ with others; freedom to worship God; ability to pray in a spiritual language; hunger to know God; joy that is too much for words and so much more!

> THE HOLY SPIRIT WANTS TO FILL YOUR LIFE.

If you're thirsty for more of the Holy Spirit in your life, do what Jesus said, *"'If anyone thirsts, let him come to Me and drink. He who believes in Me, as the Scripture has said, out of his heart will flow rivers of living water.' But this He spoke concerning the Spirit, whom those believing in Him would receive..." John 7:37-39, NKJV.*

NOT FOR THE FAINT

The Christian life is truly an adventure of godly exploits! Maybe you've heard things like, *"God has a wonderful plan for your life!"* or *"Jesus wants to give you an abundant life."* or *"Becoming a Christian is a blessed life and full of joy and freedom."* All of these things are true indeed. After all, Jesus preached the gospel, which by definition means: good news! It certainly is good news to be forgiven, favored and filled with the life of God.

However, sometimes we don't hear the rest of the story. While being a follower of Christ, a born again believer, a redeemed sinner, a saved saint and a faith-filled, Spirit-empowered Christian is the most blessed adventure God offers, it comes with its own tests, challenges and opposition. The minute you are transferred from the kingdom of darkness into the kingdom of God—you enter a spiritual battle. That's why you must decide early on in your walk with the Lord that no matter what comes along, you are going to *be* a Christian. You have to decide that not only are you up for the *love, joy and peace part* of being a Christian, you're also all in for the *in this world you will have tribulations, resist the devil, fight the good fight of faith and stand strong in Jesus' Name part* of being a believer.

Let's talk about some of the things you need to know to live out this Christian adventure. Being a Christian is not for the faint or half-hearted. It's not for wimps. If being a Christian was easy and for the weak-hearted—everyone would be a Christian! To be a follower of Jesus, you have to be willing to stand up and step out!

Being a real believer is more than the greatest sounding theory you've ever heard—it's a new lifestyle for those who want everything that comes with the adventure of following Jesus! It's not for people who want to please men and live on the fence. It's not for people who want to call themselves Christians on Sundays but live like non-believers Monday through Saturday. Being a real Christian is not something you do *accidentally* or *part-time*; it's a life you live with God—on purpose.

YOU HAVE TO BE A TOUGH COOKIE

To be a successful, fruitful Christian, you have to be a tough cookie! If you will stay close to the Lord, He will give you all the power you need to be strong. This is important because it takes His grit, strength and faith to resist temptation. It takes guts to be humble. It takes a real man or woman to love the unlovely. It takes godly determination to push through the pain of trials and tribulations. It takes tough skin and a tender heart to be laughed at, mocked and made fun of for your faith. It takes determined focus to remain undistracted by the lures of money, sex, fame or the high life. Being a Christian is not for the delicate or those who want to be popular, politically correct or praised by the world.

BEING A CHRISTIAN IS NOT FOR THE DELICATE.

Jesus painted a real picture of what it takes to be an effective Christian when He told us the Parable of the Sower. The Sower sowed the seed of God's Word into the hearts of four different kinds of people. Only one of the four people produced any lasting fruit. Let's take a look, *"Now listen to the explanation of the parable about the farmer planting seeds: The seed that fell on the footpath represents those who hear the message about the Kingdom and don't understand it. Then the evil one comes and snatches away the seed that was planted in their hearts. The seed on the rocky soil represents those who hear the message and immediately receive it with joy. But since they don't have deep roots, they don't last long. They fall away as soon as they have problems or are persecuted for believing God's word. The seed that fell among the thorns represents those who hear God's word, but all too quickly the message is crowded out by the worries of this life and the lure of wealth, so no fruit is produced. The seed that fell on good soil represents those who truly hear and understand God's word and produce a harvest of thirty, sixty, or even a hundred times as much as had been planted!" Matthew 13:18-23, NLT.* Make sure you're the type of person who hears, understands and produces good fruit!

YOU WILL BE MOCKED AND REJECTED

The Christian adventure will include persecution. Count on it. At times, you will be mocked and rejected. *"Yes, and all who desire to live godly in Christ Jesus will suffer persecution," 2 Timothy 3:12, NKJV.* To be persecuted is a compliment from the devil. In many parts of the world, when a person confesses Jesus as Lord they know it will cost them their life. Persecution is a reality in this anti-Christ culture. In the western world, persecution is not often reflected in beatings or loss of life, but when you are ostracized, mocked, rejected, dismissed or made fun of—that's persecution. When it happens, just smile and be happy.

Jesus said, *"You're blessed when your commitment to God provokes persecution. The persecution drives you even deeper into God's kingdom. Not only that—count yourselves blessed every time people put you down or throw you out or speak lies about you to discredit me. What it means is that the truth is too close for comfort and they are uncomfortable. You can be glad when that happens—give a cheer, even!—for though they don't like it, I do! And all heaven applauds. And know that you are in good company. My prophets and witnesses have always gotten into this kind of trouble. Let me tell you why you are here. You're here to be salt-seasoning that brings out the God-flavors of this earth," Matthew 5:10-13, MSG.*

THERE WILL ALWAYS BE HATERS.

There will always be haters. Our culture encourages it—even celebrates it. When your faith causes people to say mean things, exclude you, ignore you and talk behind your back—be happy, you have proof that you're like Jesus. Rejoice!

YOU WILL BE POLITICALLY INCORRECT

It takes a person of great courage, integrity and faith to speak the truth and live out the true Christian life. It's often easier to embrace a lie, a false report or a politically correct myth rather than the truth.

When you declare that Jesus is the truth—and the only way to the Father, some people will call you intolerant. When you proclaim the truth of God's Word as the standard for your values and faith, some people will criticize you for being narrow-minded and old school. When you take a stand for right and wrong—those who don't want the truth will ostracize you. When you point to heaven after a touchdown or basket, people will say you're a zealot. When you mention Jesus, put up a cross or pray in His Name at a graduation ceremony, some people will go ballistic trying to find a law to ban it. Jesus said these things would happen.

"If the world hates you, remember that it hated Me first. The world would love you as one of its own if you belonged to it, but you are no longer part of the world. I chose you to come out of the world, so it hates you. Do you remember what I told you? 'A slave is not greater than the master.' Since they persecuted Me, naturally they will persecute you. And if they had listened to Me, they would listen to you," John 15:18-20, NLT.

LOVE GOD. LOVE PEOPLE. You cannot always be a strong, Jesus-loving, Bible-believing Christian *and* politically correct at the same time. You will not be able to have the praise of man and the praise of God on every issue. It will be tough at times. So, what should you do about all of this? Walk with Jesus. Be strong. Believe God. Share the Word. Let your light shine.

LET LOVE HAVE THE FINAL WORD

Finally, let's wrap up the *7 Basics* with the greatest thing of all: love! As you live out Christian adventure—persecutions and all—you will need a *go to* place. Your *go to* place is love. The deeper your roots grow in God and the stronger they become, the more you will experience

God's love towards you and through you. As you get to know God, you will know love. As you get into the Bible, you will experience love. As you get real in prayer, you will follow love. As you get into a good church, you will share love. As you get excited to tell somebody about Jesus, you will give love. As you get your head on straight, you will flow in love. As you get ready for an adventure, you will live by love.

At the end of the day, your Christian life can be boiled down to this simple truth—love God and love people! *"So, chosen by God for this new life of love, dress in the wardrobe God picked out for you: compassion, kindness, humility, quiet strength, discipline. Be even-tempered, content with second place, quick to forgive an offense. Forgive as quickly and completely as the Master forgave you. And regardless of what else you put on, wear love. It's your basic, all-purpose garment. Never be without it,"* Colossians 3:12-14, MSG.

The greatest passage on love is found in 1 Corinthians 13. As we finish up the *7 Basics*, this would be a good passage to read and apply every day! *"Love is patient, love is kind. It does not envy, it does not boast, it is not proud. It does not dishonor others, it is not self-seeking, it is not easily angered, it keeps no record of wrongs. Love does not delight in evil but rejoices with the truth. It always protects, always trusts, always hopes, always perseveres. Love never fails."* 1 Corinthians 13:4-8, NIV.

7 WAYS TO LOVE OTHERS

Do be patient and kind.
Don't be envious, boastful, proud or rude.
Don't dishonor others or seek your own way.
Don't be easily angered or keep a record of wrongs.
Don't rejoice in evil; rejoice in truth.
Do protect, trust, hope and persevere.
Don't ever give up.

YOUR ROOTS ARE STRONG

Congratulations on completing the *7 Basics*! I pray you've gotten to know the Lord better and I trust your spiritual roots have been strengthened to grow deep in God. I hope you revisit the Scriptures and content of this book often to remind yourself of these seven important basics.

Never forget, Jesus loves you and the Lord has a great plan for your life. With a strong root system and God on your side, you are ready for a successful and fulfilling Christian life. *"What then shall we say to these things? If God is for us, who can be against us?" Romans 8:31, NKJV.*

SCRIPTURES TO READ

___ John 15, 16, 17
___ Romans 4, 8
___ Hebrews 11, 13

STUDY GUIDE

Please review the previous chapter and use this Study Guide to journal the things you are learning about the Christian adventure.

1. Have you been on any faith adventures lately? In other words, are you believing God for the fulfillment of any particular Scriptures in your life? If so, which ones?

2. What types of things does the Spirit-filled life include?

3. Why is it necessary to be a tough cookie?

4. Have you experienced persecution in your Christian life? If so, how did it feel and what did you?

5. What does walking in love look like in your life? Are there any particular people you need to purposefully love? In what ways are you choosing to love them?

FINAL WORDS:
WHAT ELSE DO YOU NEED TO KNOW?

Being a Christian is more than just an instantaneous conversion - it is a daily process whereby you grow to be more and more like Christ.
Billy Graham

There are a million other things you need to know! The whole rest of your Christian life—on earth and into eternity in heaven—will be an adventure of getting to know God the Father, Jesus and the Holy Spirit. He has a lot of revelation knowledge to share with you on many things. As you grow in your faith, you will have questions and want to know what the Bible says about all kinds of things. That's good! It's a normal part of healthy growth. As you stay in the Word, continue walking with the Lord and seek out the godly counsel of those who are mature in the Lord, God will answer your questions.

LOTS OF QUESTIONS

You may have questions about God's will on these types of things.

What makes Jesus different and what about other religions? Jesus said He was the way, the truth and the life; so it's important to understand what that means. The way to recognize anything counterfeit—including religions—is to be an expert in the truth. The more you know about Jesus and the truth of His Word, the more effective you will be in understanding Christianity and in explaining your faith. *Books of the Bible to Read: Isaiah 53, Matthew, Mark, Luke, John and Revelation.*

What should I do with doubts and how can I be strong in faith? Although doubts are normal, Jesus tells doubters to believe. The best way to starve doubts is to feed your faith with God's Word. Faith comes from hearing God's Word. As you read the Bible, His thoughts will fill your heart and mind. Before you know it, you'll be a person of great faith. *Books of the Bible to Read: Mark 4, 11, Romans 4, 10 and Hebrews 11.*

What about heaven and hell, the end of the world, the antichrist and the Armageddon? In light of our changing world, there is a lot of interest in these topics. I encourage you to read the Bible and seek out good counsel from those who have been walking with the Lord for several years. *Books of the Bible to Read: Joel 2, Daniel, Ezekiel, 1 Thessalonians 5 and Revelation.*

What about water baptism, communion, confession and other symbols of our faith? These are all important components of our faith in Jesus and His Word gives us God's guidelines on these things. *Books of the Bible to Read: John 6, Acts 8, 1 Corinthians 1,10 and 1 John 1.*

What about the gifts of the Spirit, speaking in tongues, miracles, visions and the supernatural realm? God is a God of the supernatural; with Him all things are possible. Jesus' life and ministry was full of the Spirit, miracles and the supernatural power of God. The New Testament is loaded with insight on these topics. *Books of the Bible to Read: John 7, Mark 16, Acts, Ephesians 5, 1 Corinthians 12-14 and Galatians 5.*

What about partying, drinking, drugs, addictions, pornography, and all types of sexual activity outside of marriage? We live in a promiscuous, partying, sex-crazed culture. As a Christian, you need to know how to live in the world and not be of the world. The more you learn about being filled with God, His Spirit and His Word, the easier it will be to navigate in a culture that idolizes these bondages and addictions. *Books of the Bible to Read: Proverbs 5-7, Proverbs 23-29-35, 31:1-7, Romans 1, 1 Corinthians 5-6, Galatians 5, Ephesians 5, 1 Peter and Revelation 21:5-8.*

What about demons, angels, spiritual warfare and the authority of the believer? The Bible gives us a glimpse of the invisible spiritual realm—both the kingdom of God and the kingdom of darkness. Believers need to understand who they are in Christ, the power of Jesus' Name and the authority He has delegated to believers. *Books of the Bible to Read: Isaiah 14, Ezekiel 28, Ephesians 1, 2, 6, Philippians 2, Colossians 2, James 4 and 1 Peter 5.*

What about health, healing, eating and wellness? According to the Gospel accounts, Jesus spent one-third of his ministry time healing people. The writer of Luke and the Book of Acts was Luke the physician. Jesus is very interested in the well being of His followers and the Bible is filled with balanced wisdom on this subject. *Books of the Bible to Read: Psalm 103, Proverbs 4, Matthew, Mark, Luke, John, Acts 10, Romans 14, 2 Corinthians 10, James 5 and 3 John.*

What about marriage, family and parenting? Society is doing its best to change and reshape God's definition of a family. The Bible has a lot to say about God's plan for marriage, family and parenting. *Books of the Bible to Read: Genesis 1-2, Proverbs 5, 6, 7, 31, Colossians 3, Ephesians 5 and 1 Peter 3.*

What about finding your gifts, leadership and serving God? As soon as you become a Christian, God sees you as a leader. He has chosen and ordained that every Christian produce fruit in and through their lives by discovering their God-given gifts, serving others and becoming the leaders He has called them to be. *Books of the Bible to Read: Proverbs, Romans 12, 1 Corinthians 12, Ephesians 4 and 1 Peter 4.*

What about success, money and stewardship? God wants you to do well in life. The Bible has a lot to say about success, stewardship and generosity. *Books of the Bible to Read: Deuteronomy 8, Joshua 1, Psalm 1, Proverbs, Matthew 25 and 3 John 2.*

What about God's purpose for your life—His destiny, calling and God-given potential? God has a plan for your life. You are His Masterpiece and He has ordained good works for you to walk in. Each person has been given unique gifts, talents and callings. One of the joys of the Christian life is discovering your God-given purpose and spending your lifetime fulfilling it. *Books of the Bible to Read: Psalms, Proverbs, Ecclesiastes, Jeremiah 29, John 15, Acts, Ephesians 2, 4, 1 Timothy 4:12-16 and 2 Timothy 2.*

KEEP WATERING YOUR ROOTS

You will likely have questions throughout your Christian life and thankfully, with the Holy Spirit's help, you can find the answer to every question in God's Word. The Lord has so much He wants to reveal to you, and He will do it when you are ready. You can rest in that. Jesus said,

"I still have many things to tell you, but you can't handle them now. But when the Friend comes, the Spirit of the Truth, He will take you by the hand and guide you into all the truth there is," John 16:12-13, MSG.

While having questions is very normal, don't get so sidetracked with all of your questions and desire for deep revelations, that you miss the joy of truly knowing the Lord. Always remember, the most important part of the Christian life is simply: knowing Him! *"And this is eternal life, that they may know You, the only true God, and Jesus Christ whom You have sent,"* John 17:3, NKJV.

I encourage you to always stay close to Jesus, keep watering your spiritual roots with God's Word and may the Lord bless your life and use you mightily!

SHARE IT!

Now that you're rooted in the *7 Basics*, let me encourage you to help others *get it*!

I challenge you to prayerfully consider giving this book to ten people who could benefit from a stronger foundation, deeper roots and a richer relationship with God.

For you and your technologically savvy friends, we offer an enhanced ebook version of the *7 Basics* for digital readers.

Whatever format you prefer, I pray you are encouraged and inspired to share the good news and these basics with others!

For more information, visit:
www.jeffandbethjones.org

SPECIAL THANKS

My Family: Thank you for sharing your constant love and support. Thank you for accepting the call of God on our family and for understanding the life of a writer—especially during seasons when I have to spend extra time on the computer.

Those Who Have Watered My Roots: I am indebted to many wonderful pastors, teachers, Bible study leaders, colleagues and fellow Christians for teaching me the basics and strengthening my spiritual roots. Thank you for helping me *get it*!

Valley Family Church Staff: You're the best. Thanks for your overall support and encouraging comments. I am blessed to be part of such a great team.

Tara Danielle: Thanks for being the best Personal Assistant we could ask for!

Valley Family Church and Getting a Grip on the Basics Students Worldwide: Thank you for giving me the honor of teaching you the basics for the past several decades. It has been one of the biggest joys of my life. Thank you for your comments, questions, emails and letters.

Janelle Arnold, Brooke Hovenkamp: Thank you for your attention to detail in editing this book.

Prayer Partners: Thank you for praying out the track we run on!

Partners of Jeff and Beth Jones Ministries: Thank you for believing in God's call on our lives. Your prayers and financial support are enabling us to publish the good news and help people *get* the basics!

ABOUT THE AUTHOR

Beth Jones and her husband, Jeff are the founders and Senior Pastors of Valley Family Church in Kalamazoo, Michigan, planted in 1991 and named by Outreach magazine as one of the fastest growing churches in America in 2009 and 2010. They also lead Jeff and Beth Jones Ministries, an organization dedicated to helping people *get* the basics. Beth and Jeff have four children and they make their home in the Kalamazoo area.

Beth grew up in Lansing, Michigan and was raised as a Catholic and at the end of her freshman year in college; she came into a personal relationship with Christ through the testimony of her roommate. It was there, at age 19 she realized God's plan for her to preach and teach the gospel through writing and speaking. She has been following that call ever since.

Beth is the author of 20 books; including the popular *Getting a Grip on the Basics* series, which is being used by thousands of churches in America; has been translated into over a dozen foreign languages and is being used around the world. She also writes the free, daily email devotional for thousands of subscribers.

The heart of Beth's message is a passion to help people get the basics of God's Word! Through down-to-earth teaching, she inspires others to follow Jesus and live out a faith-adventure marked by God's fingerprints!

Beth attended Boston University in Boston, MA and received her ministry training at Rhema Bible Training Center in Tulsa, OK.

For more spiritual growth resources, please visit:

www.jeffandbethjones.com

NOTES

NOTES